IMEA

IMEA

MAKING PIVOTAL MOMENTS

MIA IMEA LEE

NEW DEGREE PRESS

COPYRIGHT © 2021 MIA IMEA LEE

IMEA

Making Pivotal Moments

ISBN   978-1-63676-851-9   *Paperback*

            978-1-63730-191-3   *Kindle Ebook*

            978-1-63730-295-8   *Ebook*

This book is dedicated to my grandfather, Tong Lee. He, unfortunately, passed away during the beginning of the pandemic at the end of March 2020. People always asked me what the hardest thing was about the start of COVID-19; this was it.

Even though his passing was difficult and unexpected, in a way, he guided me to continue his legacy. Back in the day, he wrote a book while he was still in Korea, and now, I'm continuing his craftsmanship legacy.

He has inspired me so much through his knowledge as a professor and when he escaped the Korean War. He not only gained his freedom and risked his life, but he gave my family and me, as well as the future Lee generation, a chance to live the American Dream.

He taught me the importance of my Korean heritage and the importance of fighting for what you believe in. Even though my grandfather is not with us physically, he's here with us in spirit.

My family and I also never got a chance to say goodbye when he passed. This book is not only helping people pursue their peace, but it's also allowing us to say our piece with an everlasting hug like the one we lost out on.

Grandpa, I love you with all my heart, as does each family member of the Lee clan. We will miss you, but we know you'll be our angel in heaven. Thank you for your sacrifices and hard work, which allowed us opportunities today in America. Most importantly, thank you for teaching me everything from the value of respect within myself and others to being authentic on my life journey.

CONTENTS

———

INTRODUCTION

———

Imagine. You're going into your first year of college and feel the excitement of the new opportunities that lie ahead. Classes begin and seats are filled with unfamiliar faces. But as the professor starts his lecture, you begin sinking into your chair with boredom. You wonder if it's just the professor or your major, so you talk to your counselor. It's clear that this isn't meant for you, so you switch majors. Next thing you know, it's not a right fit, so you end up switching schools. Again, it just doesn't feel right. You shake it off and pretend that it doesn't bother you. Fast forward a couple of years, and you realize that college might not be for you. Sheer panic is an understatement, but it's better to take that risk than to live a lie and satisfy other people.

That's what happened to Brooke Sheridan, founder and creator of Nuri Brand. With her primary focus on jewelry creations and graphic design, she took the world by storm and forged her own path. Even though the move was risky, she was ballsy enough to believe in herself and her company. Initially, this idea terrified her, but now she lives to the beat of her own drum with no regrets, only hustling to succeed.

That sacrifice is now a trophy of honor to achieve her goals, and her story needs to be heard.

Everyone has a plan, even if they're not on the college or career route yet. From Brooke's story and from my own life experiences, I've learned that sometimes life isn't a set, linear path. It can throw unexpected curveballs in your way, but how you pivot truly makes the journey incredible.

You shouldn't be afraid of pivots but should embrace them because, either way, life doesn't give you a choice. However, you have the power to choose how you react and use those experiences to create the best outcome for yourself.

For those who don't know me, I'm Mia Lee. Before I begin, I just want to say, "Hey, everyone." I hope you all are having a splendid day filled with good energy. Thank you for taking the time to pick up my book and read this little intro. I'm an optimist and I want people to have a fulfilled life because I believe there is enough success to go around for everyone.

I created this book filled with stories, inspiration, mistakes, and, of course, pivots because we are all characters in life. You have to think about yourself as the main character in your own story to succeed. We create the dynamic and the outcome of our story. It's up to you to take life by the reigns and become an unstoppable force of nature.

My life hasn't been easy. I've struggled with anxiety, a reading disability, and various unfortunate life events. But I've learned to pick myself up along the way. Just know that you're not alone in your struggles. I know each person's challenges are different, but I want this book to encourage you not to let anything or anyone stop you from being you.

I wanted to start this journey not for clout or the prestige that comes with authorship—but to let people know they're not alone in whatever they're struggling with, whether it's their first time doing an interview or trying to figure out the next step in their career journey.

I'm just going to be real with y'all: starting adulthood is challenging. Sometimes I still want my mom to help me. Sometimes I don't want to have a checklist every day filled with chores and tasks. But the beauty of adulthood is how much flexibility we have, the unlimited number of resources, and the opportunities to become whatever we want to be.

For example, the old American Dream only gave women the opportunity to become housewives and start a family. That isn't bad, but I want to try out different things before settling down. With the new American Dream, it's now socially acceptable for women to wait to get married and have kids, have a career along with a family, and pursue different opportunities. A lot went down so that women can have the opportunities to become individuals and gain new experiences past generations weren't allowed.

We've come a long way since then. It's incredible that we have so many opportunities, but knowing *exactly* what to do can be overwhelming. Currently, we have the world at our fingertips with the technological advances of news outlets, LinkedIn, YouTube, and so many more resources that many people struggled to have for a long time. These changes needed to be made, but sometimes we take them for granted. That's a problem. So many people in the past would've killed for what we have now.

I've been there to an extent, except I'm in a world where I'm between a child and an adult. During this time, it takes some serious energy to put yourself out there.

I've realized, through taking the time to understand other perspectives, that learning never stops. Seriously, think about it. When was the last time you learned something new? Last month, last week, maybe yesterday? How about all the time? It's a nonstop process. Life is filled with opportunities to grow within your failures and successes.

Cheesy? Yes. Accurate? Yes again. The first thing I recommend doing is to get out of your comfort zone. We all have one, especially when we're afraid of the future. But that initial step needs to be taken to find success your way. The harsh reality is if you don't put yourself out there, nothing will change. But taking the time to do something that scares you every so often increases your chances of living your life to the fullest.

In this book, you'll find that I refuse to be basic in any way. I encourage you all to stand up for your own originality. This may be from the way you present yourself to how you run your company, but it really makes the difference. Think about it from a consumer point of view. What do you want to see more of on the market? Why do you apply for a job (besides getting paid)? The answer is quite simple: it excites you and makes you want to learn more.

This book contains sketches and examples but no actual template for what exactly to do. It's time to start trusting your gut if you haven't yet; it's really up to you, but this isn't an easy task. I know from experiences and plenty of failures. Sometimes things won't turn out the way you expected it, but how you use those situations to your advantage makes all the difference.

This book is a safe, nonjudgmental place for you to figure out what you want to do with your life. While growing up, I always struggled with finding out what I wanted to do and how I wanted to get there. Now, you don't have to wait for that sign. It's your chance to do things differently and change the narrative of your story.

This book is for anyone who wants to change for themselves because no change is too small. It's for people who want to make an impact. It's for people who want to challenge themselves to become the best versions of their old selves, and for the people who want to learn how to step outside their comfort zone by learning more about...well, themselves!

These aren't my only snippets of knowledge, so don't worry! There will be plenty of content with concrete stories and tips to use for future reference. Keep reading to find what content speaks to you because, ultimately, it's all about what you make of it.

PART ONE

HOW WE
GOT HERE

CHAPTER 1

THE HISTORY
OF SUCCESS

———

When thinking of the word "success" alone...what comes to mind? How do you feel when you hear that word ringing in your head? What do you envision about being "successful?"

I used to think of many different definitions of success. Initially, I thought it would feel like you're on top of the world forever, almost like a long-lasting euphoria. When I was really young, I thought it was about people rolling around in millions and billions of dollars, people not having a care in the world, people living in absolute bliss, and people traveling across luxurious parts of the world wearing designer everything from top to bottom. Yes, it's definitely the lifestyle we all want to live, only that's not the true reality of success. I hate to break it to you, but the movies and TV shows lied to you.

Throughout my early twenties, I've learned that success means the opposite of the fantasy we all crave. There's no such thing as a linear success timeline unless it magically fell into your lap. Otherwise, you probably wouldn't be reading this book.

Success has many definitions. It's balancing life with work. It's also hustling to get the work done while being unapologetically yourself in the process. Success also means having to go through a series of failures to get to the one main goal you want to achieve. That's what people don't tell you about success, let alone when you become an adult. I think it's because we're all secretly afraid to hear the truth. Life is challenging and can be hard. It's always sugar-coated to make it not sound so terrifying. But I think the truth is better than fiction.

One of my favorite sayings is:

"Success is a lousy teacher. It seduces smart people to think they can't lose."

—BILL GATES

We all need to understand this. It makes you wonder, *Why do people overemphasize success instead of failures?* Medium explains the logic people tend to have when they shy away from failure, known as confirmation bias.[1] It's when you don't want to be wrong and will give up on a goal rather than risk looking foolish to yourself (and others too).

---

1   Tony Fahkry, "Why Success Involves Going From Failure To Failure Without Losing Enthusiasm," *Medium*, July 8, 2018.

On your LinkedIn feed, you always read about someone getting a certain job or internship. Kudos to them, but people don't tell you that, when you're failing, it's okay to feel the emotions and acknowledge that you're not succeeding yet. It's also another form of FOMO (fear of missing out). According to Trust Pulse, 69 percent (seven in ten) of millennials experience FOMO, and 56 percent of people who experience FOMO are ages eighteen to thirty.[2]

We've all been guilty of posting that sort of thing and feeling that way too (myself included on both accounts). So no worries or judgment at all! It's truly a process of learning and understanding that each career journey is unique. Think about it. What person has the *exact* experiences (successes, failures, learning curves) as another individual? No one, and that's okay! We're meant to have different experiences so that we can all become the authentic individuals we're meant to be. It also allows everyone to hear other points of view.

It's also about learning how to be a cheerleader for others, even if you're down on yourself. This is such an important life lesson. I found this little snippet in a Forbes article that perfectly explains the importance of having and being a cheerleader:

New research in the *Harvard Business Review* finds that while both men and women benefit from having a network of well-connected peers across different groups, women who also have an inner circle of close female contacts are more

---

2   Coral Ouellette, "FOMO Statistics You Need to Grow Your Business," *TrustPulse*, October 23, 2019.

likely to land executive positions with greater authority and higher pay, while no link was found for the success of men in terms of the gender composition of their inner circles.[3, 4]

Quality over quantity. You hear this a lot with products or art creations, but this also applies to friends. If you want success in your life, you must examine your friends and the people you want to connect with. Ask yourself:

1. Do they support your endeavors (and vice versa)?
2. Do you guys as a group talk about ideas instead of people?
3. Do you as an individual feel uplifted while talking to them before and after?
4. Do they make you feel inspired and motivated to complete your goals (and vice versa)?
5. Depending on your answers: What can you do moving forward to implement these positive habits in yourself and your inner circle?

Taking a hard look at your friendships—whether from childhood, school, or work—can give you a clear perspective of your future. Friends come and go, but it's crucial to make sure you're choosing the right people to be actively involved in your life. Remember, women must support women.

There are many moving parts to having success in your life. However, no one said it would be easy. It's about making a

3   Shelley Zalis, "Power Of The Pack: Women Who Support Women Are More Successful," *Forbes*, March 6, 2019.

4   Brian Uzzi, "Research: Men and Women Need Different Kinds of Networks to Succeed," *Harvard Business Review*, February 25, 2019.

worthwhile, memorable path and knowing there is a plan even if things don't feel ideal at this moment.

DEAL WITH IT HEAD-ON

Throughout my college career, for example, I dealt with a lot of stress. I struggled with social anxiety. My freshman year was probably the worst time, and then it started to get better. However, I still feel stressed sometimes, which is normal, because a lot goes into finding the right job, graduation, capstones, and spending those last moments between a kid and adult. I also felt FOMO in many ways, especially because sometimes social media tends to show an ideal image. In reality, perfection doesn't exist. Truth trumps fantasy.

People tend to want success right away because they want to have everything figured out. However, there's a reason for everything that happens, even if success doesn't happen...yet. It also has to do with having a lot of pressure to be successful within, especially with our family dynamics, our current generation, and as a college student, no matter your grade level.

At the time, I thought I was the only one dealing with these emotions, especially FOMO. As I get older, I've heard my fair share of friends' stories about different challenges they face. However, when I was younger, my friends and I generally weren't yet comfortable enough to share our hardships. I found out that, statistically speaking:

- 20 percent of students report going through six or more stressful experiences in the past year.

- 87 percent of students have experienced stress during their college years.
- 45 percent of college students claim to go through "more than average stress.
- 63 percent of American college students report health-related issues as the main stressor.
- Only 11 percent of students in the US sleep well.

If you check those boxes, you're not alone.[5] Don't sweat it, though! There are ways to use that stress to light a fire within your path toward success, and it has to do with conquering fear. One of my favorite role models is Deshauna Barber. She was the first woman to be crowned Miss USA 2016 as a United States Army Reserve captain. Deshauna was also the first public speaker I actively engaged with due to my interest in the pageant world, but it's also because of the way she told her stories.[6]

What I liked the most about her speeches is that, through her failures, she didn't pity herself one bit. Instead, she used it as fuel to conquer her fears into her path as a successful leader. She told a narrative with her words that felt as if you've hopped in the story timeline with her. One of my favorite quotes was in a commencement speech for Virginia State University:

> *"Do not fear failure, but please be terrified of regret.*
> *When you walk out this door into the real world,*

5   Darko Jacimovic, "18 Eye-Opening College Student Stress Statistics," *What To Become*, February 10, 2021.

6   *Goalcast*, "Deshauna Barber: One Question Changed Her Life Forever," August 3, 2019, video, 6:08).

*you'll receive a lot of shut doors, a lot of turn down
applications. You'll hear way more noes than you
hear yeses [...] Do not fear the word no, but be
afraid of the possibility of a yes that you have pre-
maturely destroyed because you decided to quit
before the clock strikes twelve. A lot of questions
will keep you up at night, but I guarantee no question will keep you up longer at night than the question, 'What if I didn't give up?'"*

This will forever be one of my favorite motivational speakers
and speeches. When I heard this back when I was struggling
in my life, it made me stop stressing about the future of my
success. Her speech and story were incredible in so many
different ways that they gave me a different perspective of
understanding things happen for a reason within your own
success timeline, and timelines happen in a particular order.
This order is no accident because when it's meant for you, it
will be yours if you work hard, put aside the fear, and keep
going no matter what.

To better understand, I chatted with Danita Young, founder
and creator of Booty Bands & Barbells. This product is tailored for women to tone their bodies and gain muscle. Initially, she began her career as a personal trainer and then
wanted to expand her expertise as an entrepreneur. However,
she experienced many challenges in her business journey as
well as social media criticism for a manufacturing error in
her initial booty band product. She got through it by using
this mindset:

"I feel like at one point in our life, we're always dealing with some sort of struggle. There are two choices every day. We can live in an easy world or a difficult world. It's really how I view this business. It can be the worst of times or the best of times [...] What drives me forward is thinking about when I'm on my bed dying of old age. Thinking back on my life and thinking: 'Did I really take advantage of everything possible with my mind, my power, and all my abilities?' 'Did I really take the action I needed to or was I just afraid and was full of fear?'"

Even though things sometimes felt impossible or unbearable in failures, making mistakes is part of the history of success. If Danita didn't pick herself back up, she wouldn't have found a support group of twelve thousand people who supported not only her business but her beliefs and her entrepreneurial spirit. Without mistakes in our lives, we wouldn't have opportunities to learn or to grow within our paths. Mistakes are a way to force us into areas we wouldn't have pursued. They are blessings that push us into uncomfortable situations meant to be part of a bigger lesson.

I've learned overall from these incredible stories and throughout this pandemic that it's better to live in your truth and not someone else's expectations. It's also okay not to succeed all the time because it means you're learning and growing within that process. Sometimes failures come into our lives for many reasons, and we have to be okay to roll with the punches even if it doesn't initially go our way.

CHAPTER 2

PIVOTAL MINDSET

———

My brain is a miracle worker. I am a miracle. I am destined for greatness. I am the best. Say those phrases aloud and write them down below (trust me on this one):

_____

_____

_____

_____

That is the first step of manifestation and believing in yourself. I learned this little snippet of wisdom during my pageant training.

With pageants, many stereotypes need to be quickly shattered. Pageants are not like Toddlers & Tiaras. Pageants are not women who are stupid or only concerned with beauty. Pageants are people who want to make a difference in the world with whatever they set their mind to by putting their best foot forward physically and mentally. There's no such thing as a cookie-cutter woman. Each one is a unique diamond in this world crafted for greatness. And that goes for you too.

I've learned so far that believing in yourself is the most powerful weapon you can ever have in any challenges you face. It takes time for sure, but it's achievable.

When I was younger, I was always down on myself. I was bullied for as long as I could remember for different reasons, and I thought those experiences would always define me. After some time, I started to work on myself, which is how I got into pageantry.

The first time I competed in a pageant for Miss Illinois USA. I had no idea what I was doing. I was comparing myself to other women, thinking: *Why am I not as successful as them? Why aren't I as fit as them? I look ridiculous. Did I say that right in the interview?* I was constantly second-guessing myself, and I wasn't confident in my own skin. That was the old, insecure Mia before I discovered the confident Mia. Now I'm glad I went through that rough patch. I wouldn't change it for the world because it made me stronger. I'm also glad I gained a different perspective and grew from it since this will benefit you as the reader so you don't make the same mistakes I did.

I definitely can tell you what I was doing wrong then that could help you now:

I was comparing myself to other people.

Not having confidence totally sucks, but it's part of growing into a leader and understanding your worth. I was chatting with Grace Yoo, founder of Sunmi Co. Her company focuses on reworked thrift finds using her own creative twist. Initially, Grace began her business during the end of her senior year in high school and continues to work for it with passion, grit, and authenticity. Her mindset is incredible because she found confidence in herself and in her business.

> *"I think that was a huge lesson that I learned over summer because from April until now, I've gained twenty thousand followers, which is insane. When I started doing my own thing and making these designs that no one else was doing, people were naturally attracted to my account. Instead of forcing people to like my stuff, they genuinely wanted to see what I was doing," she said.*

By stepping out and being yourself 100 percent along the way, you can do wonders and open doors for new opportunities. It can be hard to do, but it's definitely not impossible because this story is proof.

At the beginning of my pageant journey, I was insecure because many of the women surrounding me had real-life experience, both in the competition side and the career aspect. A study from the Huffington Post discusses how comparing yourself can have unfavorable consequences.

The *Personality and Social Psychology Bulletin* confirmed that people are less likely to reveal their negative emotions than their positive emotions.[7] At the time, especially when I didn't

---

7   Alexander H. Jordan et al., "Misery Has More Company Than People Think: Underestimating the Prevalence of Others' Negative Emotions," *Personality and Social Psychology Bulletin* 37, no. 1 (January 2011): 120–35.

place in my first pageant, I wasn't about to share my failures on any platform because I thought they would present me as weak. But I realized through writing this book that being more vulnerable creates a more organic dynamic between individuals since it's relatable.

Then I took a break from pageants for at least a year to work on myself. One day, though, something changed. In the middle of the summer during a hot, splintering day, I had just finished walking my dogs and received a message from Alice Magoto, the title holder for Miss Ohio USA 2019. She said I had the potential to apply for the upcoming pageant in Cincinnati. At first, I was reluctant because the first experience didn't go so well. I was timid during my interview, didn't practice my walk enough on stage, and encountered a few girls who were very rude to me.

Then she connected me with her pageant coach, Becky Minger. I had no idea how life-changing that mini exchange on Instagram would be. That one conversation completely changed the trajectory of my life. Now Becky is my pageant coach, but I've grown very close to her over time, and I look up to her. She taught me how to believe in myself and never give up. She helped guide me into the career I've dreamed of both in pageants and in my professional career. I wouldn't be where I am without her. If you haven't already, I encourage you all to find a Becky in your life, because having someone in your corner to cheer you on and support you it's a real game changer (and vice versa!).

She taught me that within pageants or any competitive settings, *you are competing against yourself.*

That advice blew my mind. In any situation, it's not about comparing yourself with another person and feeling down on yourself. It's about shifting your mindset and asking these questions:

How are *you* going to work on your goals?

How are *you* going to make an impact?

How are *you* going to implement good habits in *your* life?

What are you going to do to uplift *your* spirit and your mind?

I learned what Emily Weiss, current CEO of Glossier, did to better grasp the pivotal moments during her entrepreneurial journey.

> *"My advice is just do the next right thing. It's truly a journey when you're starting out and you're an entrepreneur. The next right decision, every time. Just keep thinking, what's the next right decision? And I think that helps you get somewhere and really helps you get some momentum and leads you in the places you're supposed to go. Because you cannot possibly chart that journey. You just could not map it in your mind."*

There's no such thing as a planned playbook, and it's okay to succeed on your own journey. We've all compared our lives to others. But I've learned that each person's walk is different. It's not about what other people are doing but about cheering people on, cheering yourself on. Your accomplishments, working toward your goals, and living life your way transform you into a better self.

"Best self" is not concrete; its definition is flexible. It can be about growing your confidence, building your own company, or finishing your book for the month. It's up to you how you define it.

THE PIVOT

I remember back when in-person networking sessions were happening, and I was at the Girlboss Rally at UCLA. This moment turned into a pivot because one keynote speaker said something remarkable that I will always hold on to.

"There are so many resources in today's world that it's up to you what you make of it. Many people now have everything on the tips of their fingers with just one click but don't realize the power they have."

It's true. Many of the things we have can be taken for granted. For example, both my grandparents on my dad's side escaped from the Korean War when they were younger and had to learn English when they came to the US. This was especially challenging because, at the time, unlimited Google search wasn't available; it was all concrete reading and research in the library. They had to learn this skill by watching Elmo episodes and PBS. No one gave them the easy way out. They had to learn English or not succeed. Sometimes that's just how you have to think. All or nothing.

Intense? Yeah, but that's the norm of my family. It's what happens when you live in an Asian household with people who have been through rough times and know what the world can be like. I didn't understand it at the time, but I understand it now since it teaches you to have a strong mentality. It gives you a sense of empowerment not to give up within the pivot and take up challenges no matter how difficult they may seem.

Sure, it can be described as stubborn, but I see it as a way to be stronger than life. My grandfather was like that. Using the word "was" is hard to say after losing him. Even when he passed, he is still a strong force of nature. This part of my life was especially hard because I had to balance school, grieve, find an internship, and figure out ways to make myself feel better during all this COVID stuff. Some days were harder than others because I couldn't see anyone. I wouldn't wish my pain on anyone because it sometimes felt like too much. Many other people struggled with all sorts of emotions during the pandemic. USC found that 40 percent of US residents reported feeling anxious, and 29 percent felt depressed in early April. By late May, that percentage had dropped to 27 percent who felt anxious and 25 percent who felt depressed. The survey found that one in three people said they felt lonely, up from one in five who reported feeling lonely before COVID-19.[8]

I sometimes can't even believe I got through it with everything going on. When I said in the beginning that he is still

---

8   Jenesse Miller, "COVID-19-fueled anxiety and depression peaked in early April, then declined," June 4, 2020.

a strong force of nature, I truly meant it. I experienced one of the most unexplainable, weirdest moments of my life that I couldn't make sense of.

I found out that my grandfather passed away around three in the morning. Devastated is an understatement. I was in complete shock. We planned the funeral with my grandmother a few days later. On the day of the funeral, I woke up early and found an email saying I had moved forward in the FOX News internship process. Grandpa was my first thought. When he was alive, he always watched FOX News while spending time with my family and me. He always wanted me to become an anchor for them. I thought to myself, *Wow, my grandfather is watching over me.* I didn't tell anyone because my only concern was my grandma and dad because they had taken his death the hardest. I only told my mom quietly since I wanted the focus of the day to be on family and making sure everyone was okay.

Then, as the funeral went on all day, I was able to take a break and turn on my phone. I received several emails from companies telling me I had moved forward in their interview process or had earned internship positions. See, that's what I mean. Out of all the days, I found out this news at my grandfather's funeral. I knew it was a sign because he was all about academics since he was a former professor. It was conflicting too because I had a lot of mixed feelings. I was happy about the news while I was sad because of my grandfather. I didn't tell my dad about this until a few days later. Grieving is a strange time, and each person handles it differently.

I've learned that pivots happen when you least expect them. They happen when you lead with your heart or when you're the most vulnerable, or both. It truly depends. I never expected to hear those things, *especially* that day, when all I was thinking about was taking care of my family and making sure I wasn't crying. Everything happens for a reason. Sometimes pivots aren't picture perfect. Those moments are meant to give you different perspectives of how sometimes things can't always be explained. There isn't always an exact answer like an equation; it just makes sense with no explanation needed. It's about balancing the knowns and unknowns while going with what feels right to you.

CHAPTER 3

SCIENCE OF ITERATION

———

I always wondered how people became successful. It's especially baffling when people younger than you are making millions of dollars. I kept thinking: What is their secret? How do they do it? Why can't I make as much money as they do? I used to think it was a sign that I was failing in life because success came so "quickly" and "easily" for them. Little did I know at the time that success is the opposite of quick and easy. Now I see those types of success stories as learning lessons. There's no reason to compare each other in the process. Measuring your success through the years is the best way to grow.

Intimidation and being "above" someone because of title or position is not in my vocabulary anymore (younger Mia would be so proud of my new approach). When I was younger, I thought a title meant you were above someone, but now I view those people who created success for themselves as pivot teachers, which means that they are expert life learners in the world of noes and turning them into yeses. They adapted from those initial struggles to learn how to dodge the funnel of self-pity and turn those setbacks into thriving moments in their careers.

After changing my mindset and learning about those types of success stories from people like Deshauna Barber and Michelle Phan, I quickly realized something mind-blowing. No success story is ever the same, but there is a process and formula to get everything you want in life. It's not a clear-cut formula, but it's definitely close enough. This plan begins by taking small risks and making small changes, leading to accomplishing bigger goals. Basically, from the science of iteration, what you put in, you're going to get out.

Cliche?

Yes, but it's accurate. Iteration is defined as repeating a process with intent.

- Thoughtfulness
- Genuineness
- Ambition

This is the true core of iteration. To begin your success journey, here is a small risk you need to fill out before moving forward in this chapter:

Iterate your purpose here. This can be a range from your current goals to the future self you want to become. For example, mine would be to impact women by my aura and my platform. Now it's your turn:

_____

_____

If you don't entirely know what your purpose statement is yet, that's okay. It evolves with you along with your goals, your why, and your game plan. It's supposed to change, but it takes time to learn. Iteration is a way to learn more about yourself in your style of reaction and learning how to roll with the punches. Iteration is another form of using a superpower against negativity within your mindset and other people who tell you that it won't happen (guess what? they haven't met you yet, so don't listen to those haters!). Here are some of the iteration tips that work throughout your career journey:

1. Get yourself an accountability cheerleader: According to *Entrepreneur magazine,* there are essential steps to make your mark on the world by holding yourself accountable to follow through. The best one was finding yourself an accountability partner. Having this person or group of people by your side is super motivating. In fact, seeing a group of people come together and talk about their ideas, progress, and work is inspiring. While writing this book, for example, I needed someone to keep me accountable to my goals; otherwise, I would be shopping online and watching Netflix all day. CNBC found that "sharing your goal with a higher-up does more than keep you accountable; it also makes you more motivated simply because you care what this person thinks of you."[9]

2. Don't sugarcoat it: Acknowledge your weaknesses throughout the growth process. Procrastination has

---

9 Deep Patel, "8 Ways to Stay Accountable With Your Goals," *Entrepreneur,* March 6, 2019.

definitely been one of my weaknesses. Even though you sometimes want to take the easy route, you must kick that bad habit in the butt by being real with yourself. To make progress in this journey, you have to answer these questions:

   a. What is your weak trait?

   b. What makes you continue to fuel this weakness?

   c. Moving forward, how can you work on this weak trait?

3. Start with small risks first: I learned the concept of a purpose statement in my arts entrepreneur degree. Leading with the small risks will make it easier to complete the bigger goals.

4. Own it: Each journey is unique from the next, so there's no point comparing yourself to other people. Embrace and start craving the journey. It's the most exciting part, which creates the most amazing stories for you to tell. Make the most of it and forge the path your future self will be proud of!

5. Reflect on your progress: It's essential to keep yourself accountable to follow through on tasks, but what good does it truly do if you don't address the big elephant in the room? Reflection is key to any success. Think deeply and thoughtfully about where you're headed. Take an upgraded roses and thorns analysis:

   a. What did you do well with your goals?

   b. What didn't go so well?

   c. How did this set of small risks compare with the last set?

   d. Why did some aspects thrive while others haven't yet?

   e. What do you need to change to complete the goals?

Having an honest conversation about what you need to work on is crucial in the growth period. If I didn't acknowledge what I needed to change, I would still be in the same place. I'll have to admit, though, it wasn't easy. I'm still working on this trait, but I can proudly say I have conquered this flaw by working toward the bigger goal using small changes. For example, I learned I needed a calendar and a to-do list as a part of my accountability pact. This skill is simple in everyday routines. However, given my previous procrastination habits, it has helped me keep myself accountable and follow through on tasks completely. This book has challenged me in more ways than one to conquer that big hill.

Kay Koplovitz, founder and former CEO of USA Network, says it best:

> *"You really have to put one foot in front of the other and start on your journey. You have to be comfortable that you don't know exactly how you are going to get to the results that you want to see. There is going to be experimentation along the way. And you have to be comfortable that you can think your way through and actually execute your way through to the desired outcome. I expected to be successful. I wanted to be successful."* [10]

Risk-taking is exervous energy (my own word meaning excited and nervous), no matter how big or small it is. What's important is being the change you want in your life.

---

10   Natalie Pace, "The First Female CEO of a Television Network Offers a Springboard for Other Women," *Huffington Post*, December 6, 2017.

Whenever I'm afraid of putting myself out there or what the outcome will be, I always remember that it will make a great story someday. I wouldn't be writing this book if I let setbacks define me. It's how you turn them into learning opportunities.

Kamilah Dotson, cofounder of KCD Cosmetics, went through the process of becoming an entrepreneur. The KCD Cosmetics idea initially started when she was a sophomore in college. It was her first time taking an entrepreneurship course, and early on, she was introduced to the social entrepreneurship track. She started to think about reimagining the roles that businesses can play in our society. It stemmed from an initial opinion that people spend so much money with these big corporations, and they don't pay a lot of taxes. She found that they don't do a lot in the communities to really provide value outside of providing good products. So she took it upon herself to be part of a bigger change.

"It's to make sure that our dollars really work for us in multiple ways. And then, of course, I am a Black woman, so I'm just really always passionate and interested to see different ways that we can impact the Black community."

Knowing your "why" within your iteration is how you'll make an impact in the near future. No "why" is too big or small. Those parts of your why will spark creativity and inspiration for your next big move. From Kamilah's experience as a former undergraduate student, she took the risk on herself by following the steps I previously discussed to make her iterations come true.

This success was made possible by getting other people involved, including mentors, peers, and connections, to guide her into greatness. Since Kamilah wasn't science savvy, she took Selena Asgedom, chief product formulator at KCD Cosmetics, on board to help in that department. Together, they worked to build the company from the ground up, from the product design to the entrepreneurial spirit.

Kamilah's advice from her experience growing as an iteration expert:

> *"It's gonna be hard, but go anyway. You're gonna have a lot of fear within yourself and a lot of doubt, a lot of worry, and that's okay. Listen to that, but don't act on that. It's okay to acknowledge that, hey, this is scary. This is hard, but don't ever let it stop you; don't let anyone stop you; don't let yourself stop you. Just keep going."*

It's normal to feel scared and intimidated, whether you're interviewing for the first time or building your own company empire. Acknowledging what you're feeling and taking on the challenges makes you a girlboss. I loved Kamilah's story because it's not every day one meets an incredible, genuine, and honest entrepreneur. She was one of my first interviews for this book, and she taught me so much within the science of iteration as well as the process of success itself.

I haven't experienced what she felt as a woman of color starting her own business. I would have never known about her initial struggles of learning how to use her voice as a Black woman and finding other Black business owners as potential mentors if I hadn't talked to her. Her struggles as a Black businesswoman were eye-opening.

Each struggle is different from the next person's walk of life. Talking about the struggles and being open about your challenges makes it better in the long run to iterate your purpose. It doesn't make you weak in any way. It represents strength and courage, no matter where you are in your journey.

I truly applaud and thank Kamilah for expressing those struggles to me during our first chat. Her story about beginning her business gave me a different, essential viewpoint in understanding struggles people face in the Black community as well as allyship in the workplace (which I'll mention later on in Chapter 7).

Those struggles and triumphs make her who she is as a strong, independent businesswoman. She gave me another perspective of the different types of struggles and of how she applied iteration in her life, and it makes me certain of one thing. Kamilah Dotson will succeed in everything she does because she took a chance on herself and those challenges and transformed them into an opportunity for victory. If she can do it, I believe you can too. Her story proves it.

CHAPTER 4

SMALL CHANGES = BIG IMPACT

———

Before writing my book, I feared writing itself, which is ironic now because of this path I've taken. I decided early on to make small changes before making this big leap. I struggled with dyslexia my whole life, to the point where I dreaded reading or writing. Then one day, I decided to implement music into my reading comprehension, and it changed my outlook on everything. With that small change, I learned that everyone learns differently and that's nothing to be ashamed of. It's just another way of looking at the world and problem-solving into success.

I learned that one small factor can change your outlook on life, and that applies to your career. While taking a break from doing schoolwork one night, I decided to read a book called *Broadcast Your Beauty* by Meghan Anne Bunchman.

It's about tips and tricks to be your most authentic, confident self in the TV hosting career path.[11]

Some quotes stood out and not only impacted me as someone interested in broadcasting, but also as a feminist. I also thought all you readers who will be the future leaders of your generation would get a kick out of this. Here is one quote that got me thinking about how we as women can be leaders:

> "We, as women, have been pushing for a seat at the male-dominated industry table for so long that once we get there, we forget to pull up a chair for the next female story."

Accurate, spot-on, authentic? You betcha! That's why I chose that quote because it's a lot simpler than you think, except it can easily be forgotten in the moment.

It's a relatable statement because it's true. I hate to say it, but women struggle more in this area than men do. Statistically speaking, four in five women struggle with low self-esteem.[12] But don't give your hopes up yet because of one statistic. Those words don't define your endgame. This is how you can brush off your doubts and instead raise your esteem by turning into your most confident self. I've compiled a list of

---

11 Meghan Anne Bunchman, *Broadcast Your Beauty: TV Tips and Series* (Monee: White Feather Press, 2020), 1-118.

12 Leigh Campbell, "4 In 5 Women Have Low Self Esteem. Here's What We Can Do About It," *Huffington Post*, August 2, 2016.

the best advice from my own experiences as well as information from TED Talk, INC. and *Psychology Today:*

1. Once a day or during a weekly journaling session, write down ten things you like about yourself and ten things you're grateful for.[13], [14] This helps your mind narrow down what's most important in your life while uplifting your soul. It not only helps put things into perspective but gives you the tools to acknowledge the gifts you've received internally and externally.

2. Acknowledge that you feel negative vibes about yourself. The worst thing you can do is leave those feelings hidden. It does the opposite of good, and allowing yourself to acknowledge those sad feelings makes room to move forward into a more confident, content state. What's most helpful is talking to a counselor or lifestyle coach to help you navigate those feelings.

3. Use daily positive affirmations. A simple exercise is putting sticky notes on your top, most-seen spots, such as your desk, mirror, or bedside table. I usually have a couple that say, "You're amazing in everything you do" and "Don't give up!" I recommend these spots in particular because then you see the uplifting notes as you wake up and as you go to bed. A little goes a long way to build a Queen.

4. Create a positivity jar. Now, this is one of my favorite DIY's that's easy to make! First, you'll need these things:
   f. Jar

---

13 Guy Winch, "5 ways to build lasting self-esteem, *TED TALK X,* August 23, 2016.

14 Allison Abrams. "8 Steps to Improving Your Self-Esteem," *Psychology Today,* March 27, 2017.

g. Sharpie

h. Small scraps of paper

i. Optional: Decorations for the jar (stickers, glitter, etc.)

j. In this mini exercise, you will fill the jar completely with mini slips of paper with uplifting quotes, compliments, and so forth that make you smile as you read them. I recommend reading these out loud as you pick from the jar to train your mind to think highly of yourself. I like doing this whenever I'm in a stressful situation so I can reaffirm my worth and potential. It's especially the best gift to receive when you let other people pick from the jar. That way the love goes all around for everyone to feel their best too.

- An alternate version of this is writing on a slip of paper every time something positive happens, you think something positive about yourself, or you remember a positive memory and adding it throughout the week. That way you don't have to think of all these things to add at once!

5. Create a vision board. This is a little more time-consuming, but it's just as effective as the last exercise. This one, however, got me through a bunch of hardships, especially when I was down on myself. Here are the things you'll need for your personalized vision board:

a. Blank canvas

b. Magazine scraps

c. Modge podge

d. Paint brush

e. Optional: Stickers, ribbons, you name it!

f. Manifestation is what this is all about, folks. When you want to create goals but don't know where to start, this is the best option. The best part of this project is that it's tailored to you. It can be anything you want it to be. I have at least four different vision boards scattered (college + home) so I can keep the goals in mind wherever I go. While creating all those goals in a tangible form, I felt free. Out of all the things I had to worry about, I knew I would be okay because I got lost in the creativity. Dreaming of greatness is a great escape. The vision board helps guide your dreams into reality. I think it's such a rewarding process to do this self-care for yourself, especially if you're feeling lost. This helps redirect everything, and believe me, I speak from experience.

6. Think about and elaborate on your values. I like to evaluate my top five-to-ten values every six months to see what's changed and how to redirect my life to match them. Writing this as a journal entry helps keep track of all your thoughts.

7. Let go of negativity, whether it's a habit or a person. Yep, I said it. Negativity can come from people you hang out with, such as people who put you down or people who don't like it when you succeed. Sometimes it's hard to accept it because of how accustomed you are to particular habits. Bad habits can hold you back. Let go of those negative vibes by taking those aspects or people out of the equation. It's better to surround yourself with positivity rather than feeling bad about yourself.

8. Step outside your comfort zone to combat your fears. This is one of my favorites. It's definitely easier said than done. However, those experiences make excellent stories and learning experiences.

9. Channel your alter ego. Whenever I'm not feeling confident in myself, I create a positive alternate persona.

Whatever you fear or whatever you're not strong in, that alter ego can do. For example, in high school, I was the worst at public speaking, but then I decided to take a public speaking course in my senior year. Even though at the time I wasn't the best, that's where I learned most about myself and why I began to grow stronger in who I am. So whenever I'm nervous about something, I pretend that the alter ego is my persona. Think of it as another hack to fake it 'til you make it. :)

10. Do something you enjoy. Exercising, singing, writing... it's up to you. If it makes you happy and fulfilled, it's a step in the right direction. It also gives you the chance to unleash your energy into something good and productive.

These are some recommendations to become more confident in yourself. I really like how flexible the concepts and the strategies are. These mini lessons in your life are there for a reason. These small changes help you avoid second-guessing yourself or your abilities. It unleashes who you really are.

Because of these tips, I did some research to figure out why women struggle in this area more. An article in *The Atlantic* explains the "confidence gap" between men and women. "Compared with men, women don't consider themselves as ready for promotions, they predict they'll do worse on tests, and they generally underestimate their abilities. This disparity stems from factors ranging from upbringing to biology." Sad, right? But don't throw a pity party for yourself; here's what you can do about it. I learned from this article that high confidence actually increases your ability to take action. When we as women aren't sure about decisions or actions, we end up holding ourselves back.

I tend to do this. I'm definitely still a work in progress, but I was motivated to work on this step. Some examples are using the simple word "just" or saying "I'm sorry" even if you didn't do anything wrong. You're thinking, *Oh, that's probably not a big deal!* Except it is. They are filler words to hide behind if you're not feeling confident, but I know everyone is capable of feeling confident in your own skin. On a regular basis, women face the choice of asking versus telling it like it is. I use the word "just" almost all the time, and I've probably used it while writing this book. However, *that's okay!* Learning is one of the most unstoppable forces of nature next to love. Combining your love for learning into goals you want to achieve makes it easier to create good habits for yourself.

I spoke to Olamide Olowe, cofounder of Topicals. This is like no other skincare company because it helps guide women to embrace all parts of their skin. It not only redefines the definition of beauty but gives women a chance to love their skin conditions, especially women who have eczema, severe acne, and flare-ups. Olamide discussed her big secret of managing her confidence while being humble during the process of developing her company alongside Claudia Teng.

"I just try to keep everything at a happy medium, like not too high, not too low because it changes every day; it's something new. I have tried not to let anxiety or stress change who I am."

I've learned from her insight that the smallest changes, especially changing your outlook on high-stress situations, make the biggest impact. Olamide and Claudia dealt with people saying no to their product and getting people to believe in them. Eventually, they inspired people to embrace their skin while embracing who they were as cofounders of an evolutionary company.

Turning your dreams into tangible goals while balancing expectations of the plan is something to think about. This is especially important when running a business because logistics can be hard to obtain. However, how you carry yourself and embrace ambiguity will become the biggest game changer of your success.

Any small changes you make in your life, even if it's in the way you present yourself or how you format an email, make big impacts in your own success story. Embracing all parts of you and building a foundation of confidence increases the longevity of loving your journey. Ultimately, if you want to accomplish something truly important, it's more than possible to achieve. All it takes is spending time falling in love with yourself and the journey that comes with it. Doing so progresses you to become a better leader.

CHAPTER 5

WHY NOW?

———

Let me ask you something before we proceed with this chapter...what's holding you back from accomplishing your goals? Write it down here because we'll refer to these factors later in this chapter:

_____

_____

_____

_____

Now here's the kick puncher...why are you letting those fears, worries, or doubts take control of your destiny?

Sometimes not letting the anxiety fuel our decision-making is easier said than done. Maybe it's because we're in denial of the negative characteristics we may have learned through those hard experiences. I'm guilty as charged too. However, when we do have challenges, we can be the ones preventing good things from happening out of anxiety.

Crazy, right? Thinking about it blows my mind every time. Anything can be unlearned if you take the time to do it. Now

I'm not saying it will be easy. It will be a long learning journey, but remember that it happens to the best of us.

No matter what field we're about to pursue or where we are in our walk of life, there's always the fear, self-doubt, and that little inner critic telling us what's wrong. We can be the worst critic of them all, and sometimes we second-guess ourselves and let that worry voice in our heads take control. If you continue to pursue that kind of mentality, it won't be beneficial to your success. Even if it seems like a small factor, it can take on a life of its own. All actions and thoughts you invest your time in matter.

Now here is something crazy I came across: **women** are 97 percent *more likely* to **doubt themselves** and their ability to make an impact.

That's almost 100 percent of women, on average, feeling this way, and trust me, I had to reread that statistic a couple of times. I honestly couldn't believe it. It's a problem that most women today feel even though we are capable of making an impact. I mentioned this a while back regarding imposter syndrome and affirmations, but if you don't know yet:

All women are strong, powerful, and ambitious, including you.

Women are part of the future leaders of this generation. It's about taking a stance in who you are, what you stand for, and why you're passionate about it. Whether you're going into the workforce, starting a company, or even running for president, it all matters. So why are we struggling more in this area if we possess all the qualities to take action?

When I struggled badly with anxiety, I used to let that inner voice dictate my actions. I was the queen of second-guessing myself. I used to get scared over the stupidest things, like raising my hand in class or doing a presentation. Simple, right? But my mind automatically went into the danger zone when I had to do it. I remember feeling so many butterflies in the pit of my stomach and having this angst of self-doubt giving me little confidence in myself. I was so uncomfortable with big changes because I didn't know how to conquer those fears. My younger self chose to let that doubt take hold of me and my decisions. There was no risk involved in my choices, and that was the problem. You need risk in order to grow toward success. Although I learned this a little later in life, it all happened for a reason. If I hadn't learned that lesson, I wouldn't be writing this book now.

To help you guys take action, realize your potential, and prevent the reign of second-guessing, I've gathered the best intel of the biggest side effects of doubting:

- According to Live Happy, "If **you** replay events and often wish **you** could have a do-over, **second-guessing** could be robbing **you** of joy and self-esteem.[15] Ruminating about our choices can make us feel pretty miserable."

---

15 Sandra Bilbray, "Never Second-Guess Yourself Again," *LiveHappy*, March 18, 2016.

- From NBC News, "People second-guess themselves because they think there are 'right' and 'wrong' answers or ways of doing things. Since they believe there is the perfect answer to a problem, they get caught in a conundrum of questioning their decisions and wondering if they chose the 'right' course," says Jennifer Guttman, a clinical psychologist based in New York City and Westport, CT and author of *A Path to Sustainable Life Satisfaction*.[16]
- A *Washington Post* article, specifically referencing the *Journal of Behavioral and Experimental Economics*, says that people who second-guess themselves make worse decisions than those who stay in touch with their instincts.[17] *Ouch!*
- *Psychology Today* concluded that "when we don't like it, we call it being self-conscious.[18] It can distract you from things that matter; it can make us slow and inefficient, tongue-tied and weak—a pushover since anyone's raised eyebrow can tip us easily into self-doubt."
- Based on an article by Thrive Global, psychologists Thomas Gilovich, Victoria Husted Medvec, and Kenneth Savitsky coined the term the "spotlight effect."[19] It means that people who suffer from self-doubt visualize an imaginary spotlight on them. This results in creating

---

16 Vivian Manning-Schaffel. "Here's how to stop second-guessing yourself all the time," NBC News. https://www.nbcnews.com/better/lifestyle/here-s-how-stop-second-guessing-yourself-all-time-ncna1128681.

17 Ingraham, Christopher. "People who second-guess themselves make worse decisions, study finds," *The Washington Post*. https://www.washingtonpost.com/business/2020/01/06/people-who-second-guess-themselves-make-worse-decisions-study-finds/.

18 Jeremy E. Sherman. "Ten Tips For People Who Second Guess Themselves," *Psychology Today*. Aug 19, 2015.

19 "3 Signs that Self-Doubt is Getting in Your Way," *Thrive Global*. Updated February 22, 2019.

a smaller, weaker livelihood because they think that is what they deserve. "Those who suffer from the spotlight effect don't allow themselves to do what their hearts and minds desire. They're worried that critics will judge them, coworkers will gossip, or that their decision will cause the worst to happen; in an effort to not be embarrassed, they stay as far away from the light as possible."

Now, here's what you can do to boost your confidence and minimize those annoying doubts in your mind:

1. Trust yourself: A *Bustle* article had such incredible points on building your leadership skills.[20] This comes from taking small decisions leading up to the big risks, taking the time to learn from your mistakes and developing a mentality of being easy on yourself. You must accept all parts of you to become better and stronger in who you are, so why not start now?

2. Fully invest in your needs: Think about the essentials that can trick your inner critic to shush when it's absolutely necessary. *Inc.* magazine suggests that you need to talk to someone you trust, get active by walking or running to ease your mind, write word dumps, read other works, and listen to what others have to say.[21]

3. Understand why you feel that way toward yourself or your work: Acknowledging your feelings and telling your inner critic to shut up rewards you with deeper knowledge of how you can take control back, according to *Psychology*

20 "Ways to Stop Second Guessing Yourself," *Bustle*, last modified June 5, 2016.
21 Steve Blakeman, "5 Simple Ways to Quiet Your Annoying Inner Voice," *Inc.*, August 26, 2017.

Today.[22] Learning the root of the issues improves progress toward your positive mindset. It helps to come up with a positive affirmation to teach your brain to think like a leader.

If I had known how those doubts and critiques played out when I was younger, I would have gotten it together sooner. It's kind of crazy how one small change in your thoughts and actions can form into something bigger. These bad habits can unintentionally affect long-term plans if you let it. It's crucial to take the time to unlearn those habits so you can start your goals now. It only takes a small bad habit to wreck your chances of making positive changes in your life. Not taking care of your mind can chip away your chance of following through your goals.

When I was younger, I used to second-guess myself all the time because I didn't have confidence in my abilities or in my persona. Even though that period in my life wasn't exactly the brightest, here's what I learned:

1. No one can make the change. Only you can. I wish there was a magic wand to grant all the wishes in the world and make all the obstacles go away. But as Augustus Waters in *The Fault in Our Stars* said best, "Life is not a wish-granting factory." The world doesn't owe you anything. You owe yourself the chance to take a risk on what you believe in, including who you want to be.

---

22 Lisa Firestone. "Steps to Overcoming Your Critical Inner Voice," *Psychology Today*. May 21, 2010.

2. Stop apologizing. I'm guilty of doing this, and I'm still unlearning it, since it can easily be a trapped, comfortable habit. The next time you catch yourself apologizing for no reason, think about why you're doing it. If there's no relevance, kill it with confidence.

3. A period of time isn't forever. It can be challenging to think about that sometimes when you're dealing with hardships. Thinking about the future is the only way you can break out of the rut cycle.

4. Think about and acknowledge why you feel these things. It's important to reflect on moments, good or bad, to move forward in life.

5. Your feelings are valid. You are valid. Don't let second-guessing yourself stop you from achieving greatness. It's okay to be human about these things because these moments will help guide you into your future

6. If you don't do it, will you regret it? Whether you succeed or fail, it's about the fact that you put yourself out there. You made a change for yourself, and that's something to be proud of. It would be bad if you didn't take that leap of faith and regretted it when it's too late. As Nike puts it, Just Do It.

7. Squash your inner critic. Although having a conscience can be good to make thoughtful decisions, these thoughts shouldn't take total control of what you want to do.

It doesn't matter how fast or slow you're making progress. All that matters is that you're making this monumental progress for *you*. I bet many things influence your actions, but this stems from having confidence in yourself because you possess the qualities of being an ambitious leader. That's the biggest part of the *why now* factor. All of these steps are toward a better successful future for yourself.

In an interview, Sophia Amoruso talks about how she became her girlboss self using tactics called the Girlboss Oath.[23]

> *I will live deliberately. I will work with intention, play with intention, and love with intention. I will take nothing at face value, ask questions, and write my own rules. I will wake up every day to fight the most important battle of my life: my life. I will be curious and trust that, in time, my questions will answer themselves. I will play my strengths, sniff out my shortcomings, and stomp out my ego at every opportunity.*

This oath is one of my favorite quotes and the perfect example of a positive affirmation. It's not only pure genius from the one and only Sophia herself, but it helps your brain recognize who you will become, developing a deeper sense of self-confidence and leadership.

Another favorite quote I always go back to stems from believing in yourself and what you're capable of:

> *"The **first secret** of success: **Believe in Yourself.** Nothing changes in your life until you **believe** you can do things that are important to you. And if*

---

23 Zameena Mejia, "3 pieces of career advice Girlboss founder and CEO Sophia Amoruso wants you to know," *CNBC.*_

*you have a low opinion of **yourself**, nobody else is likely to raise it."*

With everything you absorbed in this chapter, look back at what you put down initially and put a positive spin on those doubts:

_____

_____

_____

_____

_____

Confidence is like the sun rising. It needs to glow from the outside and the inside in order to produce the right amount of sunshine each day. Remember that.

PART TWO

PRINCIPLES OF THE REDIRECTION MINDSET

CHAPTER 6

IMPOSTER SYNDROME

———

While writing this book, I felt like I was an imposter. Usually, when I thought of people writing books, they were older, with their whole plan and everything figured out. I'm pretty young, and it's kind of freaky thinking about it. I also thought I needed to experience certain life events first, like having a job. But here I am, writing this book. Then I wondered why I suddenly felt insecure about myself and my work ethic.

Ah, yes...the infamous imposter syndrome, a psychological pattern of feeling doubt about your accomplishments or talents. It also has to do with internalized fear of being exposed as a *"fraud"* or *"fake"* in your position or achievement. I've also learned that this is common with women in particular because in society women are not portrayed as leaders (which is ridiculous because we're all capable of being leaders in our own way) and shy away from being vocal within their positions.

"We're more likely to experience imposter syndrome if we don't see many examples of people who look like us or share our background who are clearly succeeding in our field," said

Emily Hu, a clinical psychologist in Los Angeles on BBC. It's said that women are less likely to be hired and promoted to manager. Yeah, I hate reading that, too.

Ladies, from one former shy girl to another, **speak up!** It's okay to say how you're feeling and to be direct with your leadership style. I'm still learning how to do this because everyone is a work in progress at the end of the day, no matter what phase they are in. It's high time for women to be bosses and stand up for themselves. Sure, men are fully capable of being leaders of a company, but women are also capable of being leaders of these companies, so don't forget that.

Society is built based on reactions and patterns a group has or encounters within various situations. With imposter syndrome, it's a systematic concept that has been built in a sociological setting way back. It's up to us to be the change we want to see in the world. And yes, I quoted Mahatma Ghandi because he had some pretty good things to say.[24] As the future of women leaders, it is our responsibility to collectively stand up for what's right and become ambitious forces of nature in this world.

I recently spoke with Raquel Phillips, cofounder of Qatch, an online personal shopping messenger. She told me how she overcame imposter syndrome while starting her own company with her sister Nicole Phillips.

---

24   Omar Itani, "8 Quotes By Ghandi That Will Change The Way You Think," *Medium*, *Mind Cafe*, Feb 20, 2020.

"It's so relevant. It's basically like women leaders, especially when thinking of entrepreneurs. They always feel like they are not good enough to lead a business or do what they're doing. And I have definitely struggled with that. I've gotten better, I'll say. Also, you grow with the time that passes. The first year of doing this, I was shy and scared and thought, How am I doing this? I'm so young! What am I doing? I don't know what I'm doing! Which is fine. It's okay to admit that you don't know what you're doing, but I mean, I put the work in. We've accomplished a lot so far. Just having that solid track record has helped me say, Okay, I kind of do know what I'm doing. We were able to grow our business this far...grow our team, grow our user base. That must mean I am worthy of being in this position. I think that's definitely helped my confidence,"

I think, within this perspective, you have to be determined that you *will* succeed. Yes, more manifestation coming your way, but I'm not wrong and I know I'm not. Cocky, I know, but I'm confident when I say this: don't let anyone make you feel like you're not fit for any position. Everyone has different walks of life, and no one can compare yours to the next person because each human being on this planet is unique.

Imposter syndrome is a lot to handle, but remember that you can only control what *you do*. It's a hard pill to swallow, especially when you're under stress. This advice will save you loads of time. I have dealt with my own inner critique of second-guessing myself. I can make a firm guess that you hate that feeling as much as I do. It's important to surround yourself with people who believe in you and vice versa, magnifying happiness, motivation, authenticity, and positivity. I truly believe that everyone deserves to feel empowered by the people around them. It's so important to find your circle in any field you pursue.

Having a circle of friends who support you is so important in your walk of life. Whether it's your girl gang or hype squad, each individual truly makes a difference in your outlook. However, I wouldn't necessarily rely on one group. In anything I'm doing, I always have different groups of friends and hype queens in my corner. I wish I had learned to do this a long time ago.

In high school, I never really had a set group of friends. I hopped around to different groups because I wanted to meet different people. At the time, it felt foreign for me to do that and like I was the only one. Now, I'm glad I did those things for myself. It's completely normal to want to meet new people and try out different things. Life is full of opportunities to do so. Limiting your horizons doesn't benefit you; it only holds you back from exposure to different backgrounds and experiences. Finding people you enjoy spending time with can be a challenge, especially during COVID-19 (stay tuned for COVID-19 tips soon), but putting yourself out there increases your chances of finding the right people for you and diminishing your imposter syndrome.

CHAPTER 7

LIFETIME LEARNERS + A GUIDE TO ALLYSHIP (POST-COVID)

I'm starting lucky number seven with the perks of lifetime learning. I purposely wanted to combine the two parts because both aspects go hand in hand. First, let's start this off right.

Jot down some things you learned today:

_____

_____

_____

_____

Then go ahead and write down some things you learned in the past (it can be anything from a setback, daily life mishap, etc.).

_____

_____

_____

_____

Finally, list some things you would like to learn in the future, both short-term and long-term goals.

_____

_____

_____

_____

I know some of these exercises seem like common sense, but this proves my point exactly. Learning never stops. It's always evolving as you get older and more in depth with your career path. This exercise is truly one of my favorites because it helps with manifestation. The Subconscious Servant article explains that "when you write, all your attention is on creating the words that you put down on paper. There has to be a strong **intent** or the energy that you're putting into them. That focused **energy** is why writing things down to manifest works."

I learned this trick when I initially joined the pageant realm. It's one of my favorites because, when time passes, you can look back and see the progress you've made. When you do look back, you'll notice that some goals were completed and some weren't. You have to think deeper about why they weren't done and then go from there. That way, you can hold yourself accountable and follow through. In terms of future goals, that depends on time, effort, and, of course, faith in yourself as well as the universe.

A favorite quote of mine truly fits into this ideal of having a goal-oriented mindset while learning:

"A clear vision, backed by definite plans, gives you a tremendous feeling of confidence and personal power."

—BRIAN TRACY, THE GIFT OF SELF-CONFIDENCE

One hack that makes these goals a reality is turning them into mini checklists every day. I do this trick regularly to complete all my deadlines in time and motivate myself. I almost turned it into a game and analysis. I ask myself:

- How fast can I get this done?
- Which one of my checklist items will I finish first?
- Which one do I need to focus on the most?
- Which tasks are a priority today?
- Why is it important to get this done today?

I also add simple checklist items like meals because sometimes, with online learning and outside commitments, I forget about time and eating balanced meals. Honestly, if I don't put that simple necessity on my checklist, my stomach growling loudly will remind me as if a bear woke up, and my energy level starts to drain like my iPhone battery at the end of the day. Regarding daily checklists, it's found that:

- "When we experience even small amounts of success, our brains release dopamine, which is connected to feelings of pleasure, learning, and *motivation* [...] Checking items off of a checklist releases small amounts of dopamine that then fuel us to keep checking off more items, i.e., get more done! Raise your hand if you've ever written a task down just to immediately check it off?"[25]
- More recently, a study by professors Baumeister and Masicampo from Wake Forest University showed that, while tasks we haven't done distract us, just making a plan to get them done can free us from this anxiety.

With that being said, lifetime learning also applies to allyship within the workplace and understanding different perspectives people have within their own cultural backgrounds.[26]

On top of dealing with a worldwide pandemic in 2020, the murder of George Floyd sparked nationwide outrage and increased awareness of racism, unjust policing, and institutionalized discrimination. But before we dive into this topic, I have to address something important: the people we've lost along the way. We mourn the loss of George Floyd, Breonna Taylor, Ahmaud Arbery, Elijah McClain, and countless others who may go unknown to the public. These injustices shed light on our past history and our present situation. Being a good ally means focusing on what we need to do better and how we can be better allies moving forward, especially in the workforce. While these events were occurring, I kept

---

25   Melissa Chu, "Why Your Brain Prioritizes Instant Gratification Over Long-Term Goals, According to Science," *Inc.*, July 10, 2017.

26   E. J. Masicampo and Roy F. Baumeister, "Consider It Done! Plan Making Can Eliminate the Cognitive Effects of Unfulfilled Goals," 1-18.

thinking to myself, *How can I support someone during this difficult period and give endless virtual hugs to be a good ally and a good friend?*

1. SUPPORT BLACK-OWNED BUSINESSES

For people not knowing where to start their allyship journey, you can always begin this process by supporting Black-owned businesses. It can be as simple as recommending a product to a friend, sending a compliment via @anysocialmediaoutletpossible, or cheering them on during their career journey. I've learned that the simple acts of paying love and respect back to people can greatly impact the long run.

Here are the companies I recommend supporting (I also encourage you to research other Black-owned companies as well because these aren't the only ones to support!):

- 28 D.Tales Media Company
- KCD Cosmetics
- Fiona: House of Femme
- JUMU brand
- Pooka Pure and Simple
- Maquillage Detroit (Ma-kee-ya-ge De-twah)
- Golden Girly Shop
- KLUR
- Thebe Magugu
- Under Things Shop
- Tree Fairfax
- Fyre Vintage
- Orchid Bohème
- Zelie for She

- Humans Before Handles
- The Lotus Bloom Co

2. ACTIONS SPEAK LOUDER THAN WORDS

Now this is important. I believe it sets the tone in allyship because it affects every minority group. For example, I am multiethnic, and I've dealt with racism, discrimination, and microaggressions, but I've also seen some of my friends encounter racism on different levels. Sadly, we live in a world where there isn't as much equality as we would like. But there are ways we can be the change we want to see in the world.

To start, here is my small list of dos and don'ts that can make an impact (+ or -).

Do these things, please, with a cherry on top:

- Never assume when referring to a person's pronouns. Ask what their pronouns are, respect them, use them, and correct yourself immediately when you mess up.
- Ask someone about their ethnicity like this: "What is your ethnicity or cultural background, if you don't mind me asking?" If a person isn't comfortable with that question, be respectful of their choices. It's also important to think about why you are asking the question. Is it relevant to the conversation or necessary to ask? Each person's preference is different and is important to abide by. Better to be safe than sorry.
- Capitalize the B in Black.
- Set aside stereotypes and understand who they are as a person.

- Acknowledge cultural or racial differences because it's better to acknowledge rather than be color-blind.
- Educate yourself. This book is good for starters, but other publications, movies, podcasts, videos, TV shows, and articles also explain topics like this from different, equally important perspectives. I will attach my top picks of those educational resources at the end of this chapter!
- If you don't know how to pronounce a person's name, ask how they pronounce their name traditionally. Keep trying to learn the correct way to pronounce it, even if it's hard. It's the effort that makes a difference.
- Speak up and have a conversation about discrimination or racism because no one deserves to feel a certain way because of their cultural background.

Don't do this unless you really want to piss someone off:

- When asking about pronouns, do not say "preferred" pronouns. In the LGBTQ community, doing so makes it seem like a personal preference rather than an identity.
- Do not ask anyone these questions, because they're offensive enough: So what are you? So, like, where are you actually from? (Yeah, I hate these questions too, because they make me, and I'm sure others, feel like an alien species. Newsflash, we're not. We're human beings like everyone else, so please refer to the right, respectful way to ask this question above.)
- Don't call someone "exotic" as a "compliment." I hate being called exotic because I feel as if I'm an animal or alien species (I'm sure other people feel this way too). If you think someone is beautiful, cool, awesome, or pretty, I recommend just saying that instead of exotic. The term

exotic itself doesn't make you feel any of those positive things; it just states that you're different from everyone, and not in a good way.

- Don't leave the B in Black uncapitalized.
- Don't compare people to stereotypes of any kind when getting to know them. Any qualities having to do with their race or background is just flat-out wrong. It's important to be aware of people's cultural background and not be color-blind, but it's also important to appreciate their qualities as a person. People want to be liked because of their personality and accomplishments, not because they're known as the token person in a certain company.
- Don't ignore a person's race or cultural background entirely. This is known as color-blindness, not with vision per se but with not taking the time to see a person's race or cultural identity. This is an issue because it doesn't address who an entire person is.
- Don't ignore racism, discrimination, bias, etc. Even if it's not happening to you, it's happening to others around you.

Ultimately, these little things can make a huge impact and impression no matter which side of the interview process or workforce you're on. "Workplace allies," according to Eli Inc., are people who are willing to personally align themselves with colleagues to make sure they're heard and included.

3. UNDERSTANDING THE GRAVITY OF BIAS

Seeing someone treated with bias hurts my heart because it's judging someone before you even know them. A study from Impact Group found that:

- 48 percent of African American women and 47 percent of Latina women report being mistaken for administrative or custodial staff.
- Less than 15 percent of US men are over six feet tall. Yet 60 percent of corporate CEOs are at least this height. The taller a man is, the more likely he will earn more than a shorter man.
- Resumes with African American, Asian, and Hispanic names are less likely to get callbacks for interviews.

I can't completely understand how it must feel for someone with a unique name or qualities to struggle with this type of treatment. However, I'm also aware of the privilege I do have because of my first name and some aspects of my cultural background, like having a lighter skin color. I'm trying to take the time to understand the gravity of bias because I want to be part of the right step in the workplace and in history. I hope from everything that happened in 2020 that you do the same. This conversation highlights the necessity of learning about other people's experiences with bias both in and outside of the workplace. It's also important to hear different perspectives on how it feels.

I had to include this snippet from Adzaan, one of my dear friends from college, which explains her process of overcoming bias perfectly.

"When confronted with this type of information about diversity and the workplace, I had to force myself to operate under the notion that in order to be successful, you have to work twice as hard just to get that foot in the door. Having a Black parent, I was told this at a very young age. There's a famous scene from the show Scandal, where Olivia Pope, who's the Black White House Chief of Staff, was told by her father that 'you have to work twice as hard to get half of what they got.' I don't know about the experience that other minorities have with this, but a lot of Black people can relate to having some form of this conversation. On one level, it does affect your sense of worth as a professional and is discouraging, but on another level, you have to turn around and motivate yourself to make sure everything is extra excellent, dotted i's, crossed t's in place for that one person who will grant you that opportunity."

4. ACCOUNTABILITY WITHOUT CANCELING PEOPLE

We're all human, and we all make mistakes. Being a better ally is about learning and becoming a better person. It's simple. A person who makes a mistake should own up to it, but sometimes people don't like to be wrong. I'm stubborn in my work ethic, but I try not to let it control my actions. If I'm wrong, I'm wrong, but I learn from it, and I take steps moving forward to avoid making that mistake again. I don't ever want to offend someone or make someone feel bad about their cultural background, and neither should you.

However, we can hold people accountable without canceling them because of a mistake, no matter how bad it is. People, including myself, aren't perfect. It's okay if learning from those mistakes takes time, which I'll discuss in the next section.

Accountability is taking responsibility for your actions and putting aside your pride so you can understand why your actions were hurtful and/or offensive.

5. ALLYSHIP TAKES TIME

People have different learning processes within their own allyship journey, and that's perfectly okay. Being an ally isn't just one and done. It's a series of things that may need more time than others. We have to understand that good things take time. Maybe someone doesn't understand how you encountered racism or discrimination. Have a respectful discussion about it so people can better understand what you're going through and how you feel about it.

This also ties into whether to protest or not. Although protesting can be a really positive and effective way to be an ally, it might not be for everyone, and that's okay, too. It's not the only way to be heard or to get your message across. There are various ways to use your platform and voice, especially with the power of social media. But with power comes responsibility. You have to realize that posting on a public forum is forever. Instead of deleting the post, admit you were wrong. Apologizing and correcting yourself publicly goes a long way.

Each individual's voice is unique and powerful. The way they use it can be just as unique and powerful as the next person. You have to find your own way to be an ally while being respectful of people's choices even if they aren't the same as yours. A person's specific action [or how they chose to support a cause] doesn't define their whole allyship journey. Judging a person based on their means of support isn't effective because they could be doing something behind the scenes we may not know about.

RESOURCES TO EDUCATE AND BECOME A BETTER ALLY

MOVIES:
- *13th*
- *Do the Right Thing*
- *Malcom X*
- *Homecoming: A Film by Beyonce*
- *Black Panther*
- *The Hate U Give*
- *Just Mercy*
- *Crazy Rich Asians*
- *Selena*
- *To All the Boys I've Loved Before*
- *Frida*
- *Love, Simon*

TV SHOWS:
- *Dear White People*
- *Do Better YouTube Series*
- *All American*

- *Stay Woke: Truth Series*
- *Asian American Docuseries by PBS*
- *Love, Victor*
- *Trinkets*
- *Ginny and Georgia*
- *Never Have I Ever*

BOOKS:

- *How to Be an Antiracist*
- *White Fragility*
- *So You Want to Talk About Race*
- *They Can't Kill Us All*
- *Minor Feelings*
- *Dear Girls*
- *What Is Not Yours Is Yours*
- *If They Come for Us*
- *Under My Hijab*
- *Generation M*
- *I Speak for Myself: American Women on Being Muslim*
- *You'll Grow Out of It*
- *Salsa, Soul, and Spirit: Leadership for a Multicultural Age*
- *The House on Mango Street*
- *Queer, There, and Everywhere: 23 People Who Have Changed the World*

PODCASTS:

- *NPR: Code Switch*
- *NYT: A Conversation with Black Women on Race*
- *BBC World: Witness Black History*
- *Slay in Your Lane*

- *Invisible India*
- *Self Evident: Asian American Stories*
- *NYT: 1619*
- *AsianBossGirl | Episode 104 with Tammy Cho & Michelle Hanabusa, Cofounders of Hate is A Virus #StopAsianHate*
- *Naptime Is Sacred*
- *That's So Hindu*
- *The DiscoverU Life Podcast*
- *The Thinking Muslim Podcast*
- *Latinos Who Lunch*
- *Outward*
- *Queer America*

CHAPTER 8

MAKING MISTAKES IS MY STRONG SUIT

———

I have frequently applied for different positions and jobs and received an answer something like:

"We're sorry to inform you that we picked another candidate."

or

"We're sorry to inform you that you, unfortunately, will not be placed to move forward in the process."

It stings, but I've realized over time that it would sting more to get a job or a position that wasn't meant for you. Regarding those setbacks, I remember wondering *why?* Now I know the reason. It's because even if a certain position is not meant for you now, it will be meant for you soon if you keep pushing yourself to achieve it.

Before COVID-19 hit, I remember feeling rejected. At the beginning of my junior year, a news company gave me an interview for an internship position. It was a huge company, and I was extremely shocked to be considered for it. There were three interview rounds, and I made it past the first one. Then came the second round, which was a hot mess.

When my phone alarm woke me up, I forgot where I was. You know when you had the most amazing sleep and felt like you were floating? That's exactly how I felt. Suddenly I remembered what day it was and felt a cramp in the pit of my stomach like a piece of paper crumpled up a million times. My adrenaline started racing as I turned off my alarm. *Snap out of it, Mia.* Then I got ready as usual and put on my makeup—brushstroke after brushstroke.

Next, I felt one heatwave after another as I finished flat ironing my hair. Before leaving for the big day, my mind went quiet and I knew what I had to do. I looked into the mirror and gave myself the best pep talk of my life. *Mia, you got this. You prepared yourself for this opportunity, and you aren't going to give up. Go nail this interview.* After a moment, I left to set up my laptop. Microphone? Check. Video? Check. Wi-Fi? Check. Stable connection? Check. As I waited for the interviewer, I was exervous.

Five minutes passed after the original interview time. *No worries,* I thought. *They're probably just running late. I'll look over my notes to be extra prepared.* Ten minutes passed. *Okay, so maybe I got the wrong time for the interview?* Fifteen minutes passed. *Have the right time slot, but where's the interviewer?* Twenty minutes passed. I called my mom in a panic:

"Hey, mom..."

"Hi, Mia, is everything okay?"

"No, it's not. My interviewer hasn't shown up for the time slot, and I don't know what to do. Should I just leave the call?"

"No, I would email them and say...."

"Hang on; someone's logging on. I'll call you back."

The interviewer finally showed up. It was the moment of truth. My interview felt rushed, and I was already flustered by the setback. I knew from that conversation I didn't get the internship.

Sometimes things don't go as planned. As much as I did to prepare for that interview, I realized I could only control so much. I was really upset because that setback threw me off; it was an unexpected variable. I never expected the interviewer to be late. I made sure I got logged in and situated ten to fifteen minutes early so I wouldn't be late. I was also disappointed about not getting the full time promised or the opportunity to showcase who I was and why I wanted to earn the position. What was supposed to be a twenty-minute interview turned into a five-minute interview. The worst part of all was the woman who interviewed me never apologized for being late. You should always apologize if you are late, regardless of your position, but she chose not to. So this was not my ideal way to be interviewed. Even though the circumstances sucked, it taught me not to let setbacks define me.

I remember my mom telling me, "I didn't raise a quitter, Mia. Follow it through and see what happens." I used to hate it when she said that because I knew she was right. There, I said it. This is every mother's dream, and now it's in my book. Mom, if you're reading this, I wouldn't admit it then, but I'll admit it loud and proud now.

You were right, Mom.

You have to hold yourself accountable and say I'm going to do well, I'm not going to give up, and I will earn the right position for me. This is another perfect example of manifestation. It's about being your own hype woman to become the person you want to be. Fake it 'til you make it, right? But seriously, there's a method to my madness. You must pin down the goal in your mind, write it down, and tell people you're close to about it leading up to the big achievement. There's no question that you *will* achieve greatness.

Have you ever heard of the saying...

"When you show God your plan, he laughs."

Well, sometimes things don't go as planned, but it could go better than expected. Claudia, the head of the Grad Soc, a program for young adults to gain skills to be better prepared before diving into the career field, told me how her experiences made her stronger in her position.

When Claudia graduated from the university, she was unemployed for about three or four months.

"I think that was probably the toughest for me," she said. "I had the best time of my life the last few weeks of uni[versity]. You're around new people, and everyone wants to have a good time. Then suddenly it's like, oh shit, like back to reality."

She was supposed to start working at a summer camp but instead launched her career at Grad Soc.

I used to hate it when I made mistakes, especially when I was younger and struggling with dyslexia. Now, I can look back and say those were small mistakes. At the time, those mistakes were my worst nightmare, and they truly felt big to me. It was definitely the worst feeling when I kept messing up while reading in front of my class(es) and wondering if people would judge me. I thought my mistakes defined me.

You're probably wondering, *hey, why would you add those negative comments in your book? Wouldn't it remind you of the bad times?* Yes, it does remind me of when I wasn't confident in myself or my learning style. However, it only has power if you let it define you. Those memories are now reminders of how strong I am because I didn't let them tear me down and define me. If you have struggled with *negative comments, do not listen to them.* Block them out. I remember my mom talking to me about the horse races and the helmets. They had to wear them in each race to block out their competitors because it distracts them during the race.

Think of that helmet in your life. Put it on when you want to block out the noise—things that aren't worth your time or energy. It can be drama, worries, pettiness, or just things that irritate you. Ultimately, it's your choice if you want to have those negative experiences in your life. Aside from the necessities, you don't have to put up with anything that drains you, that isn't good for your persona.

For example, when I was younger, a friend would make me feel drained after hanging out or after a conversation. She acted as if life was just passing by and always felt sorry for herself, taking no action to make things better. A person *should not* make you feel that way. That is not a positive way to spend time with people. It was a very toxic friendship, and no one should ever put themselves in that situation. Unfortunately, I eventually did have to put my foot down because it got to the point where I couldn't be myself or I had to hide part of myself away. No! Never, ever, dim your light for someone because they're feeling down, insecure, or whatever excuse they come up with. It says more about them than it does about you. That's why it's important to preserve your energy for something actually worth spending time on and why it's important to have a good girl gang (which I explore more in the Imposter Syndrome chapter). Block out the bad vibes and bring in the good energy.

Mistakes, in my opinion, are things you learn as you go. Especially within any writing process, making mistakes is inevitable. When I started writing for my school newspaper, I made so many mistakes. I most remember taking on two stories in one week because I honestly thought I could do it, which was not the case. I had to extend one article, and the other one was a dead-end story because I couldn't get enough interviews in time for the deadline. I hated that I couldn't do it, but that experience taught me that balance is key. Sometimes you can't do everything, which is totally okay. It's all about what you can take on your plate and playing it by ear each week, especially if you're doing other things outside of that commitment.

Sometimes making mistakes does take a toll on you, but the difference is how you use that energy toward something better. I started improving in this area, and the practice truly paid off. This was especially a big theme during 2020's pandemic. Now I know I discuss COVID-19 topics a lot throughout this book, but let's note some differences. Let's further explore how 2020 went and how we're now all moving forward in a better direction than when this event initially began.

1. We didn't wash our hands.
   a. Gross...I know. I cringe as I write this. However, now looking back, we all know how to wash our hands and to be more mindful of everyone in our community.
2. We didn't know how to use online learning.
   a. Yeah, this was a tough one, too, and I truly hated it when I started all my classes online. Now, all of us have a better idea of managing our time to do well in school and being proactive within our career paths.
3. We wanted to socialize...except that wasn't even a possibility.
   a. This is still difficult with the pandemic still going on, but I have faith that we'll all get stronger in this department. I've been going to online events to be engaged and meet new people. I've also been hanging out with select people who aren't sick and who are following the COVID-19 guidelines (like y'all need to).

CHAPTER 9

HELP + STEPPING OUTSIDE YOUR COMFORT ZONE = PROGRESS

─────

Lately I've been asking for a lot more help. I didn't do it as much when I was younger because I was always afraid I would look stupid. Over time, I grew out of that fear. If it doesn't work out, it doesn't work out. If it works out, great! Currently, I'm not ashamed of or afraid of asking for help because it's part of life. Without it, we would all be doing stupid stuff 24/7. Asking for help better guides you in any process.

In a study by The Great Work (conducted by the O.C. Tanner Institute), Forbes found that 72 percent of people who receive awards for their work ask for advice, help, insights, and opinions from people outside of their inner circle. [27] Taking advantage of your resources and using them to understand different perspectives will open doors for your success.

This skill is especially resourceful for finding your career path and asking for help doesn't make you weak. It gives you a better perspective of your goals and what it takes to get there. It's also an opportunity to step outside your comfort zone. Although comfortable can be nice, comfortable doesn't make you successful. Risks motivate you more to succeed. An Entrepreneur article states that "taking risks eliminates the possibility of looking back and asking, 'What if?'[28] Even if you fail, you'll walk away with more experience and more knowledge, which can lead you to further success in other areas, and at least one study shows that risk takers end up more satisfied with their lives because of it." [29]

I have a vision board on the side of my window with the phrase "Full Speed Ahead" next to a graphic of a woman getting ready to run while looking stylish. I thought of it as being unstoppable in your pursuits, not turning back even if you made mistakes along the way and looking fabulous while doing you. It motivates me, and I hope it motivates you during your endeavors.

---

27 David Sturt and Todd Nordstrom, "4 Reasons Why Asking For Help Makes You A Stronger, Not Weaker, Leader," *Forbes*, November 7, 2017.

28 Sam McRoberts, "Here's What Science Says You Should Do to Achieve Greater Success," *Entrepreneur*, December 29, 2017.

29 Jennifer Warner, "Are Risk Takers Happier?" *WebMD*, September 19, 2005.

I did a little research to see what inspires people to take big risks and stumbled across multiple articles about Sara Blakely, founder of Spanx. An INC. article shared how her Spanx creation was called "so crazy."[30] It's even crazier that people underestimated her, and now Spanx are in stores everywhere. What I did find crazy amazing is her mentality during her risk.

Recently, I went to a bustle career networking event (online). Initially, I thought it would be super serious and formal, but it was quite low-key. There were almost two hundred girls on the Zoom call, and I thought I would hear the same-old advice: use LinkedIn; learn how to find the right internship for you. However, I was wrong again.

I learned more about what it takes to make a pitch to a publication, how to follow up with people within your interested field, and how to be original while standing out in your writing. Overall, the team had a variety of women with different backgrounds and career paths, which made me genuinely love the company's platform. It made me remember why I wanted to go into fashion. No role is big or small. Each role is personalized for what you want to get out of it. Teamwork makes the dream work, and delegating tasks is part of the job no matter what role you're in. The end result is totally worth it.

Listening to what everyone had to say from both sides of the panel was such a cool experience. It gave me a better

---

30 John Rampton, "Businesses That Took Huge Risks That Paid Off," *Inc.*, October 11, 2016.

perspective on what companies were looking for and knowing that we all were experiencing exervous energy. I also didn't expect to connect with so many amazing women who were extremely supportive and uplifting. We created several different group chats and connected on LinkedIn to learn more about each other.

If I hadn't asked for help and signed up for the event, I wouldn't have learned and met those incredible women. In anything you do, you always learn something new, no matter what. Even though it can be scary and intimidating to put yourself out there and test the waters, it's worth it. Honestly, I *know* I would have regretted it later on if I didn't (virtually) go. The best advice in this book is you won't know unless you try. Think about it. Many things can go wrong, but many things can also go right. It's all about switching your mentality to trick your brain into taking more risks.

Attending events can sometimes be nerve-wracking for me. I struggled with anxiety as a child, and later on, as I got older, I figured out that I was struggling with social anxiety. In the past, I was really shy and didn't talk to many people. Now I can definitely say I've outgrown some old habits by working on those skills. However, every once in a while, the old habits creep in. Comfort is the best way to describe those habits, but not anymore though. Your comfort zone can figuratively kill you. I use a few different tricks to turn off those little fears:

1. Listen to fun bops—songs, if you will—to pump up with a positive momentum.
2. Journal about the fears to let out all the anxious energy.
3. Stretch with a little meditating.

4. Give myself a nice, old-fashioned pep talk.
5. Put my fears aside and *doing it.*

Whether it's a pep talk or a positive attitude going into it, each choice you make for yourself is crucial. I believe everything in life happens for a reason. Nothing is by accident. I've learned that nothing will change if you keep making the same decisions. Choosing to grow and keep trying despite the challenges makes you bound to go a step further to be the person you want to be.

According to neuroscientist Dr. Tara Swart, our current risk aversion or risk tolerance is linked to how we've benefited from risks in the past. If you take a risk and it pays off well, you physiologically respond by favoring risks in the future[31] The opposite is true if a risk doesn't pay off.

Raquel Phillips, cofounder of Qatch, shared her authentic but uplifting experience with the initial start of the business:

> *"I have not been taking a salary for a year and a half. I've completely sacrificed a lot of my time and obviously like earning money, saving, and having a normal twenty-five-year-old life where I don't have the responsibility of running a business. But that's the sacrifice I made, and I knew I had to be persistent and keep going down this path if I wanted it to work. It's tricky. I feel like when you get into*

---

31   Vivian Giang, "You can teach yourself to be a risk-taker," *BBC News*, June 6, 2017.

the business, there's gonna be some sacrifices you have to make."

When stepping outside your comfort zone, you must be aware of the sacrifices you'll make along the way. Raquel's experience reminded me that sometimes taking risks won't be peachy keen. Sometimes it will be challenging, especially within the financial department. Whether it's going into an interview for the first time or starting your own business, you can't turn a blind eye to those aspects. You must understand all angles of each risk through a positive and negative lens. However, I believe that everyone has the entrepreneurial grit to accomplish their goals if they want to. The more you fail, the more you're likely to succeed. Taking the time to do this for yourself is crucial. Balancing the sacrifices and risk-taking can't be overlooked.

A few ways to balance those aspects is by:

- Planning
- Not Being Cocky
- Learning
- A Hint of Optimism
- Being Okay with the Uncontrollable

This combo can be hard, especially when it comes to failures. However, those five little tips make a big impact in the long run. Sure, you can take one and not follow the others, but combining them all into your process equals powerful results.

PLANNING

Planning takes time and allows you to step out of your comfort zone. Reflecting on your wants, needs, strong suits, and areas of improvement is key. According to Chron, "The planning process provides the information top management needs to make effective decisions about how to allocate the resources in a way that will enable the organization to reach its objectives.[32] Productivity is maximized, and resources are not wasted on projects with little chance of success." The time is now to seize it.

NOT BEING COCKY

One of my pet peeves is someone being arrogant instead of embracing humility. It's okay not to know everything. No one said it was required, so, from the bottom of my heart, please don't act like it is. You can have the hustle mentality in your mind to be your own hype woman, but doing it too confidently is a major turnoff as an entrepreneur and in building connections with other people. Confidence is not cocky. I define confidence as knowing who you are and knowing how you will handle a situation, not by knowing everything but by knowing yourself.

Being cocky is bluster, insecurity, and the fear of being vulnerable.

---

32 Brian Hill, "The Importance of Planning in an Organization," *Chron News*, February 12, 2019.

LEARNING

Learning is a cycle of life, and so is asking for help and stepping outside your comfort zone. As a baby, you learn the basic functions of behaving and acting. Then, as you grow older, you learn the essentials of education and so forth. Learning evolves every day. Remember that learning is different for everyone, and it's a daily function.

A HINT OF OPTIMISM

No one likes a pessimist or naysayer—people who are pessimistic because what you're doing isn't the "normal" thing. Being a Debby Downer is not the way to go, especially when wanting to succeed. Not being optimistic during the risk process sets you back, but it can be unlearned. Instead of "I can't do this," say, "I can't do it yet, but I will learn these skills to do better." This trick encourages your brain to have a more positive outlook while acknowledging the doubts.

BEING OKAY WITH THE UNCONTROLLABLE

Not everything can be planned. When experiencing setbacks, it's okay to take time for your wants or needs, especially if you're feeling down. It's even okay to ask for help. When I feel bad about a failure, I give myself a little bit of time to acknowledge how I'm feeling, take time to process those feelings, and pick myself back up to move forward. Any uncontrollable aspect can be nerve-wracking, stressful, and annoying.

Remember that everything happens for a reason. Think of a setback as an opportunity. I always love to refer to the saying if a door closes, a window opens. It stuck with me, and I hope it sticks with you if you're ever struggling. Things work out if you let the universe in.

CHAPTER 10

THE PIVOT

———

I became familiar with pivoting when life forced me to get out of my comfort zone. It's within your entrepreneurial spirit and is always being learned.

"I define a career pivot as doubling down on what is working to make a purposeful shift in a new, related direction. Pivoting is an intentional, methodical process for nimbly navigating career changes." [33]

—JENNY BLAKE

The best way to understand pivots thoroughly is by knowing the difference between change and transition within a pivot. Indeed says it best: "Change refers to the situations or events that happen to people and organizations.[34] It is external and not always something they agree with, although it can be. Transition, on the other hand, is the internal

———

33 Jenny Blake, "When To Make A Career Pivot," *Forbes*, September 9, 2016.
34 "How to Adapt to Change in the Workplace," *Indeed, Career Guide*, last modified December 10, 2020.

process of adapting to a situation that is new. It is the process of successfully adapting from an old way to a new."

As the challenges get bigger, I've come to realize that so do the changes, transitions, and, most importantly, the pivots. This is true of anything related to your life, your business, and your brand. These pivots all start with you. The pandemic has definitely challenged people to make those changes. People either adapted or neglected the inevitable. There's no in-between because people either enjoyed staying in their comfort or decided to take risks even if it meant failing. Pivots were the big theme in 2020. Can you guess what I'm talking about?

If you never heard the word COVID before, you probably live under a rock or on another planet; this is all anyone talked about in 2020. COVID-19 affected the economy and job placements overall, which were lower than the Great Depression. That is extremely scary to think about. It affects so much of our livelihoods from the education system to the workforce. COVID-19 is on everyone's minds because it determines so much of our now and our future. It's crazy to me how time flies. Before the pandemic, we were living in fast motion, needing to know our schedules ahead of time for events, career planning, and so forth. Now we live in a time where things are so unknown and mysterious that it's almost the norm not to plan ahead at all. For the remainder of my senior year, I had many mixed feelings. Seniors just wanted to graduate but didn't know if there would be a job for us when we did.

These are some things I encountered during this time, and I'm certain I'm not the only one:

- One: Everything is remote, and there are barely any in-person classes for the fall semester of 2020 (hopefully it won't stay that way). It's weird because we all grew up learning in person, but now that has completely changed.
- Two: There are various options for jobs and internships since everything is online. Remote work (full– and part-time) and events are available since no one wants to get sick or to get anyone sick accidentally. I've read different discussion boards and talked about this with several people. Before COVID-19, everything was only in person. Barely anyone I knew was doing remote work except for my good friend Adzaan, who is pursuing a career in graphic design.
- Three: It's up to you to get stuff done. Yeah, that's usually the general rule of thumb for any task, but for some reason, doing it online feels totally different. "Online classes offer more efficient learning because you don't have the lag of a group class. It depends on how they learn. If they can motivate themselves, then online is a great option," said Tiffany Ellington, an undergraduate studying in digital audiences at ASU. If you feel strange doing education or work online, you're not alone.

The pandemic will be one of the most historical events in our lifetime. I rooted those experiences from my learning journey and other people's experiences.

For example, my friend Hannah Valdez had to figure out how to find an internship. She was moving forward in her dream internship role, and then they canceled it due to the pandemic. To pivot she promoted herself by being honest and authentic. I remember when everyone was losing jobs and internships from left to right. Many individuals used social media because that was the only avenue of communication. In-person events were all off the table, and everyone (including myself) was under a lot of pressure. Hannah's story is relatable because she didn't give up despite the obstacles.

When I came across her LinkedIn post about her struggles in finding an internship, I thought: *Wow, she is such an ambitious woman, being unapologetically real and authentic. I'm thankful I'm friends with someone like that.* Putting yourself out there even if it highlights the struggles makes the difference. It shows that through the challenges, you *won't* give up. Hannah ended up totally clapping back at COVID-19 and doing three internships at the same time.

It's okay and normal to feel anxious, depressed, or unmotivated through this time because it's overwhelming. Students have so many more options to choose from than previously. Whether it's deciding to take a gap year to do an internship during the pandemic or continuing your educational journey remotely, it's about customizing the time to make it useful and exciting in the long run.

For anyone wanting to branch out into a remote internship or integrate themselves in the freelance world, now is your chance. At first, I thought anything remote was completely taboo and out of my range of expertise, but now I love it. You don't have to worry about commuting or putting too much effort into daily routines like getting dressed in the morning. However, it definitely isn't too easy, especially when you're balancing different online classes and maintaining your motivation. In my experience, it truly takes practice.

In the summer of 2020, I held three different positions. If these opportunities were in person, this never would have been possible. God works in mysterious ways.

I worked a remote job as an editor for a boutique media group, as an editorial intern for a fashion magazine, and as a fellow in the author fellowship program. I also worked on this book throughout the pandemic. On top of that, I was taking fifteen credit hours to complete graduation requirements so I wouldn't have to worry about fitting those classes into my fall or spring semester. It was definitely a plate-load, and I had to sacrifice my summer, but it was totally worth it. There was no perfect time other than the pandemic. The virus was still very much unknown, and everyone was pretty much inside quarantining out of fear of getting sick.

I sometimes don't even know how I did it, but I kept telling myself *I wouldn't fail* by any means necessary. My biggest tip for anyone working this type of schedule while being a full-time student is that calendars and to-do lists are your best friends. They help keep you on track and organized to get everything done. Technology definitely helps because I relied heavily on my Google Calendar and the notes section on my laptop because that was where I could communicate the easiest with my various groups and positions. Organization apps are also available to keep yourself accountable like Click-Up, Quip, or Asana. It takes time to figure out what works best for you, but it's also an opportunity to sharpen your time management skills. A lot more goes into it than you think.

I initially had a hard time adapting to online learning with my dyslexia IEP (Individualized Educational Program). I *had* to figure out how to work efficiently while balancing my lifestyle because students across the world had no choice with the pandemic in our midst. In retrospect, this was a challenging adjustment in many ways. I usually prefer in-person classes because I'm a hands-on, visual learner. Most of my classes were interactive, with group work and arts courses, since I'm pursuing a creative field (journalism, fashion entrepreneurship, photography). So some things were not meant to be online, like my entrepreneurship and photography classes. That was the most difficult for me because, at the time, my creative juices were on pause after losing my grandfather during the middle of the semester. It took time to regain that strength, but those struggles meant I learned something from the experience, and that's what matters. Even though some classes were able to adjust during the pandemic, some, unfortunately, were harder to adapt to.

Here are some of the tips I used frequently to stay on top of my A-game and take care of myself within the pivotal changes:

1. It's okay to fail.
I'll say this once and say it again: failing is how you learn! For the longest time, I used to feel so ashamed and embarrassed whenever I failed at anything. Little did I realize that failing is crucial for success in any path you take. The *Harvard Business Review* agrees that "failing early and often is a Silicon Valley cliché. But the key is to fail as cheaply as possible."[35]

---

35 Caroline O'Connor and Perry Klebahn, "The Strategic Pivot: Rules for Entrepreneurs and Other Innovators," *Harvard Business Review*, February 28, 2011.

Failure is the gateway to self-discovery. It teaches you how to embrace more ambiguity in your life and roll with the punches no matter where you are. Even though some challenges truly are the worst, you become stronger. What doesn't kill you makes you stronger! So seriously consider a time when you failed but really *succeeded.* Write it down and reflect.

_____

_____

_____

_____

2. Determine your learning style.
Whether it's for classes, internships, or jobs, learning is always evolving and is an unstoppable force. It's helpful to take a work personality quiz to think about your strengths, weaknesses, and work style. To make it more interactive, you can even do it with your friends or with a group of people to get to know each other more and work more efficiently the next time there's a big project.

3. Find ways to normalize your routine.
Saying that is weird because this whole COVID-19 situation is completely abnormal. To keep a good momentum, find ways to have a consistent schedule to complete your work while not burning yourself out in the process. This means considering how much screen time you have, how much off-screen time you have, how you're maintaining a balanced lifestyle, and how you're finding ways to make yourself happy. Harvard Pilgrim Healthcare says you have to focus on the quality of your screen time, ask yourself what kind of positive activities the screen might be replacing, and set up realistic

rules for your household. But remember to go easy on your-self—we're all just wading through uncharted waters.

There are many things like the pandemic that you can't control. However, you can control what you do. So how will you adapt to the lifestyle you want to achieve? Following are the top events that impacted our mistakes, our learning curves, and our pivots:

1. Networking is a _____ (fill in the blank of how you feel about it)
   - This is definitely a struggle because of the decrease in formal handshakes and in-person events. We're handling Zoom etiquette better than before and are using our social media platforms to connect with other professionals (and soon-to-be professionals!).
2. How to live your life during COVID-19
   - This is an unknown aspect because, as a society, we want to plan things ahead of time (myself included). It's truly mind-boggling that there is no set plan. However, I think now we're improving on rolling with the punches and making the best out of each situation.
3. The loss of jobs and internships
   - The job market has been scarce and is sometimes still a struggle because we haven't fully recovered yet. I think now, there is more hope and better support for people to find job opportunities.
4. The recession
   - The last one was around 2008–2009, and I was almost ten years old when my family and I went through that. Although I don't remember much, I remember

that we had to be mindful of our expenses and what we chose to spend money on as consumers. This current time in our history teaches all of us how to be smart with our money, and it's always a learning experience.

5. George Floyd and Black Lives Matter
   – This was truly a learning experience for me, and I'm sure for others as well. I have known racism and discrimination as someone who is mixed, but I took some time to educate myself through the lens of the Black community. There were things I knew, things I didn't know, and things that I'm still learning about. Each process is unique to a person's walk of life. However, these events surrounding racism and police brutality made us more aware of our actions and the actions we need to take to be better allies and a better community. Along with the pandemic, those events are the most important, lifelong experiences of them all.

I can't and will not ignore these events. I chose them because they showed differences within our generations from Gen Z to baby boomers. We learned our strengths and weaknesses through those events. Although we all never expected them, we become stronger because of them.

Sometimes the most vulnerable things that happen are our wake-up call to be better people and go after better things in life. It applies to everything that has happened to us. It's impacting us at this very moment in time. In retrospect, not everything will be perfect. It's what you make of it.

CHAPTER 11

THE BIGGER PICTURE

———

Nothing in life is constant, especially when things don't go your way. Failures and setbacks are challenging. I never understood how hard finding a job was until I had to do it myself. The most challenging part is doing it during a pandemic. Many jobs are scarce, and so many people are trying to find jobs at the same time as everyone else. Getting those rejections and going through those series of emotions can even take a toll on confidence. Throughout my job search, I've received many rejection emails saying they found another candidate or don't believe that I'm a good fit for their position. It's difficult now, since I'm about to graduate, but I know in the long run, I'll find something great.

That's the mindset shift you need to instill within yourself—the bigger picture, as people call it. Those small setbacks don't define you. You define yourself by getting up from those challenges and pushing through to become successful. During the start of COVID-19, Kate Davis, founder of Knockout Inc. (an amazing ring collection to keep you safe), opened up to me about the struggles she encountered during the peak of the pandemic.

Initially, before social distancing was a thing, Kate attended trade shows regularly to get her brand out there and promote her product. After a major quarantine mandate, she was forced to stay inside, and all the trade shows she planned to attend were canceled. Then Kate struggled with her accounts. At the time, she was expecting eight accounts to fully stock her ring products in their stores, except that never happened. The accounts were left unpaid, and the stores retracted their initial orders because they didn't need them anymore.

Talk about a whirlwind of problems! Things started looking up when she received a grant, which allowed her to upscale her jewelry, photography, and website and gain consistent sales.

"I think having a mission-driven business makes it easier to reach people across platforms, whether you're in person or online, because if somebody resonates with your mission, then they don't need to know you, necessarily. But I love in-person events," said Kate.

Whether you're a business owner or not, we all sometimes want things to be easy. However, if Kate hadn't gone through that rough patch, she wouldn't have learned more about her bigger picture as a business owner and within her mission. After her updated launch, she caught the one and only Sophia Amoruso's attention with her ring company. Now she's moving her way up in the business world, and I couldn't be more excited for her! By taking reins of the setbacks, she came out stronger than ever while successfully branding her business. I'm really lucky I met someone who gave me the scoop of what it's like to be a business owner during times of uncertainty.

She also shared how she coped with the initial fear of not being good enough, especially within the craftsmanship of the creation. Just the other day, one of my art professors asked, "Does it bother you when you showcase your work and someone might not like it?" I said no because I use those critiques as motivation to do better. That skill took time for me to learn.

Learning how to shake negative remarks about me or my work wasn't easy. It doesn't happen overnight; believe me, I've tried. In the modeling and pageant world, critiques are going out left and right. It's especially bad with anonymous internet trolls who don't care if you're hurt. Unfortunately, that's part of the business and the reality of social media.

Even on my writing path, I've grown from where I initially began. All the critiques in that sphere began early on when I was struggling with dyslexia. Now that I'm fully immersed in the writing field, my feelings of rejection or embarrassment have lessened. I've learned that it's all a part of your growth. Picking up on this learning curve made me more conscious of curation. It's knowing before you walk in the door that people may or may not like you or the work you do. That's life, but I'm urging you not to take it personally.

That's the big game changer. Once I removed the personal side, it became easier to detach from those feelings of insecurity. I've also learned that there are two types of people when looking at the bigger picture. Some people help you because they want to see you succeed, which are my favorite kind people. Others intentionally make you feel bad about yourself or your work due to their self-esteem issues.

Over time, I've learned how to differentiate the two within my creative avenues and turn my own thoughts and outside opinions into motivation. Having multiple opinions is good, especially when you want to improve. However, balancing the constructive critics versus the negative criticism is a must. You can't surround yourself all the time with negative connotations because it would put even the best of us in a bad headspace.

It's all about listening to what's right for you and knowing that you'll get through the rough patches.

To simplify the bigger picture along with the benefits of switching into this mindset, I provided a curated list from *Entrepreneur* magazine:

WHEN LOOKING AT THE BIG PICTURE, ASK YOURSELF THE FOLLOWING THREE QUESTIONS:

1. Why are things occurring as they are?
2. What is really necessary?
3. How do the various single pieces with which I'm involved fit into the grand scheme of things?

THREE BENEFITS OF LOOKING AT THE BIG PICTURE:

- It allows you to see opportunities for improvement.
- It allows you to communicate that big-picture view to the rest of the team.

- It serves to reinforce the real reason for the activities you do daily.[36]

Taking a good look at your current life situation and spirit will help you move forward in your personal development. Remember to only focus on what you can control. Many external and internal factors can steer you in the wrong direction if you don't take control. Listen to what is necessary and forget the rest if it doesn't help you or others.

Plus-sized influencer Chenese Lewis discussed how she made her mark.[37] At the beginning of her career path, she began looking into her brand and finding innovative ways to shatter the glass of ideal beauty. Chenese was working with what she had while being grateful for the journey. As a child, she looked up to public figures such as Queen Latifah, Mo'Nique, and Oprah Winfrey to forge her path. This not only created a blueprint for successful Black women making their way toward success but allowed Chenese to build herself up.

"I created opportunities for myself when others weren't [....] I had to learn how to do basic graphic design, website building, writing contracts, and public relations for myself," she shares. "It would have been easier if I had a team to do all these things on my behalf, but I didn't have the budget. I took the time out to learn the industry standards, and I became extremely conscious of always

36 Phil Geldart, "The Importance of Seeing the Big Picture," *Entrepreneur*, April 30, 2020.

37 Virgie Tovar, "Meet One Of The Original Plus Size Influencers," *Forbes*, October 13, 2020.

presenting myself in the most professional way pos-
sible so I could compete with people who had more
resources than me."

By doing those things for herself, she knew what the bigger picture meant. Chenese became one of the first influencers in the plus-size space way before *influencer* was an official term. Her actions meant inspiring women, especially Black and plus-sized women, to know that anyone can succeed no matter who you are. Success comes from grit, hard work, and not letting society tell you who you are. One of my favorite quotes ties into Chenese's story really well:

"Never tiptoe through life, babygirl. Let them hear every step you take."[38]

—@BUSINESSWIFEY INSTAGRAM PAGE

Knowing when you need to make a change for yourself is one of the most stressful things. We're so accustomed to staying in our comfort zones, but that's not how we accomplish our goals. It's certainly not how we find the bigger picture. There are ways to slowly uncover the big picture.

1. Don't get stuck: This is probably one thing that can stop us from achieving our goals. When I'm upset, I feel like I can't move, but do you want to know the trick? Give

---

38 (@businesswifey), "Never tiptoe through life babygirl. Let them hear every step you take," Instagram photo, October 14, 2020.

yourself an hour to feel bad for yourself and get back up and start again. Life won't stop because you're not happy with the way things are turning out. Acknowledge how you're feeling, accept that things aren't going your way now, and then get back up. Things *will* go your way by working hard and not giving up on what's most important to you.

2. Make an "I want" list: I learned this trick from a CNN article.[39] It gives a few tips and tricks for adapting your brain to think more toward the big picture and less on minor aspects. An "I want" list is a confidence booster that will keep your goals aligned in your pursuits. Whether it's landing your dream job or building your company empire, this list keeps you in check. Another tip is to be confident and not shy away from it. As career coach Corrine Mills says: "That's your time to say, 'This is where I see my future heading.'"

3. Hype yourself in your head, but don't be cocky. *Elite* magazine said it best: "It's important to be confident in yourself and know your worth, but don't be cocky within the process."[40] Wouldn't you find it very rude if someone thought they were "It?" I think it's super irritating and annoying when people get big-headed about their goals, acting as if they've already got it. It's definitely not the first impression you want to leave. You don't need validation from others to know who you are or approval on your wants. Ultimately, you have to be happy with your decisions.

---

39 Rose Hoare, "How seeing the big picture could bring success, fulfillment," *CNN*, August 30, 2012.

40 Olly Joshi, "29 Ways To Remind Yourself To Keep Sight Of Life's Bigger Picture," Elite Daily, February 10, 2014.

These decisions to obtain big-picture thinking are up to you and only you. On my Instagram feed one day, a caption read, "Positivity is a choice." In reality, you choose everything you do each day, whether it's the food in your mouth, your behavior, or your actions. Make each decision count, learn from those experiences, and taste the zest of life. You'll thank yourself later for making those choices because you won't have regrets. I'll leave you here with one of my favorite quotes:

> *When you are able to see the big picture and realize what is actually going on, you will quietly and calmly become the master of your own life. Your thoughts, feelings, and behaviors will carefully calibrate themselves with clarity, peace, understanding, and truth in order to define a happy life.*

PART THREE

HOW TO GET THE REDIRECTION MINDSET IN YOUR CAREER

CHAPTER 12

ENTERING THE WORKPLACE

———

I'm not here to sugarcoat this experience because you deserve to hear the truth. Entering the workplace is hard, but it's definitely not impossible. All you need is confidence, a killer resume, a thoughtful cover letter, and one heck of a good impression.

No application is the same. The most important thing is it depicts who you are. Potential employers don't want a cookie-cutter candidate but someone they can visualize working and getting along with well, especially within a team setting. Sometimes we can easily forget that someone is on the other end of the application. We get so caught up in the stress and narrowing down detail after detail. Paying attention to detail is essential, but it's not the only important aspect to consider.

It all comes down to the human touch of what makes you... you. Whether it's a font you use or a story, this is your time to shine. Here are some of my go-to tricks to make your application stand out:

1. Motivation for the nation: Thinking about what drives your excitement will give an idea of your passions. What do you like and dislike? I guarantee you can't fake it. We all need to be paid, but put that aside. It's not about getting a job you hate. Passion will make you feel excited about the work you're doing. Don't forget that.
2. For all my creatives, add some flavor: Even Forbes magazine agrees with me on this one.[41] The standard resume is great for beginners, but a resume should evolve with you. This includes, but is not limited to, the font, design, and craftsmanship. No basic details allowed. Make it tasteful while showcasing what you got.
3. Reflect on each decision you make: Yvonne Agyei, chief people officer at Bookings.com, reads at least four hundred thousand applications a year, and she's seen it all. Being purposeful and genuine in all aspects of your application will make you stand out.
4. For the love of God, please research the company whose job you're applying for: A while back, I was on the other end conducting interviews with my former coworkers for our internship program. While I watched the round two live interviews and videos, it was obvious who studied and who didn't. Save yourself from embarrassing yourself ahead of time. Doing research on the company you're passionate about shows you care not only about the job but enjoy their content, product, or work. It also good

---

41 Melanie Haselmayr, "5 Creative Ideas To Make Your Job Application Stand Out," *Forbes*, September 5, 2013.

conversation for the interview. Please do yourself this favor.

5. Have hobbies outside of the potential job, internship, or position: I build a portfolio and have a section of hobbies to showcase all parts of me. Another amazing article from *Forbes* magazine mentions that you want to be memorable during the interview process.[42] Interviews can be based on feelings, so make those connections, stay true to your brand, and stand out.

How do you feel when you see the word "Interview?" During the process, you encounter several different personalities and the same annoying poker face the interviewer(s) put on so you don't know what they're thinking. Poker faces are probably the one thing that irritates me during interviews because I rely on facial expressions to understand what a person thinks about me.

I like that I'm curious, and it's also what makes me ambitious. I wish people could be real with me when they don't think I'm right for the role. It's fine! I'd rather know now and rip off the theoretical Band-Aid rather than slowly but surely peeling it off. I'm sure I'm not the only one with this train of thought in interviews.

Think about the person not as an employer but as a thinking, feeling being. Do you think they laugh maniacally and like to say "no?" Do you think they want to reject potential

---

42 Expert Panel, Forbes Human Resources Council, "14 Effective Ways To Stand Out From Other Applicants," *Forbes*, June 15, 2020.

employees? Does it totally make their day when they interview a bad candidate and get to ghost them?

1. Categorize your thoughts.
After a certain number of interviews, you begin prioritizing your interview jitters. It's more important to be less focused on the poker face and more focused on the questions. You can do this mentally or by writing down your worries. Put the priority in a big font and the nonessential in a small font so your brain can have a mental vision of what's more important. It's okay if this method doesn't work right away because practice makes perfect. It took me some time to categorize the worry and become my best self, but learning paths are unique on any scale, which I'll explore later.

2. R E L A X. (Doesn't this make you feel relaxed just reading this?)
You can combat interview jitters by doing something that relaxes you before you begin—whether it's listening to music, doing some zen meditation, or giving yourself a mental pep talk to be your most confident. I've done all the above whenever I'm nervous for an interview.

I'm sure everyone is wondering what to do if you don't have time to relax or prep. Ah, the last-minute interview.

Well, story time. I was talking to my friend Adzaan Muqtadir the other day about her life.

Adzaan moved to NYC in late July. She was optimistic about the NYC bubble, filled with the glamour, adventure, and quirks the city has to offer. It was her goal to move there when she finished her undergraduate degree, and she found an apartment right near the heart of Brooklyn. After she got settled in, she began applying for jobs to branch into the real-deal NYC lifestyle and waited some time to hear back about her applications, Now brace yourselves...this is where the craziness begins.

Adzaan slept in a little that day because she had been at a party the night before. She checked her phone but didn't have any alerts. Then at 11:20 she found an email for an interview that had been scheduled, but the recruiters had sent the email too late.

"So that's where I got that little adrenaline shock to the system and got the phone call from the recruiter, who said, 'Hey, we messed up. We're still gonna do the interview but it's gonna be at twelve,'" Adzaan said. She rushed into overdrive, desperately trying to do some research and refresh herself on her personal script before the interview.

I can feel her adrenaline as I read her words. It's probably the worst interview nightmare I've ever heard of, but sometimes it's what you make of it. Even though it was *completely* unexpected and she had little time to prepare, Adzaan handled it like a champ!

Instead of focusing on what could go wrong, think about what will go right. You are the main character, and you are in charge of your destiny and no one else. Crazy, right? This took me some time to learn, but I'm a firm believer in growth as well as manifestation.

Growth happens when you're out of your comfort zone because it allows you to put yourself out there and make it happen. Now this is where manifestation comes into play. It's the ability to pursue your goals, not your dreams, and bring them to reality. Goals have specific steps and are created to measure accomplishments, while dreams are fantasies that don't require work. There's a big difference.

I truly admire Adzaan's because finding out your application moved forward isn't an ideal situation. She took it as an opportunity to hone into her strengths and put her best foot forward no matter how short the notification period was.

3. Interviews are like formal conversations with *practice.*
The word interview itself terrifies me to my very core. I was able to relax beforehand by acting as if it was a conversation with a family member. This tactic gets the nerves down and makes for a more thoughtful interaction between word choices and the stories you want to bring up. But don't forget that practice makes perfect!

According to Glassdoor, you should gather the most common interview questions and have at least a few notes for each one. Having a list of your main points and practicing will make a big difference in your delivery, especially during Zoom calls. Be sure not to memorize every answer. It can come across as too rehearsed and fake. It's also helpful to get other people to practice with you.

With a couple of my mentors in the fashion community, I would talk about interview prep and do mock interview sessions with them to keep those skills fresh. It helps to get feedback regarding improvements needed and your strengths. It's also helpful to record yourself if you want to try it solo. Nothing too scary! I promise! If you're still in college, take advantage of the career center. I know everyone says that, but it's there for a reason. I used the career center all the time for advice on resumes, interviews, and so forth to get a different perspective. These people have the experience and words of wisdom to help you toward success.

CHAPTER 13

WORKPLACE VIBES

———

You landed the job! Congratulations! Now it's time to buckle down and learn what it takes to be a killer worker bee. This comes down to understand your boss, including the different types of bosses you may encounter; having stellar communication skills; being an accountability queen; and learning how to bond well with your coworkers while getting stuff done.

First things first, understand your boss. You get through the interview and are so stoked to get started. Moving forward, thinking about the type of boss you have and will be working with is crucial. Here's a list of different types of bosses we may encounter within our career paths:

1. The Title Hogger: This person loves their job position almost too much and has a "because I said so" mentality. A way to pique their interests and get the job done, according to Business Insider, is balancing what they ask and what you think is right.[43] Just know you can't change

———

43 Heather H. Huhman, "15 Types Of Bosses And How To Work For Them," *Business Insider*, June 3, 2013.

their behavior, but you can control your actions. Bottom line, don't do something ridiculous or compromise your integrity because your boss says so.

2. The Workaholic: This person works, eats, sleeps, repeat like they're the energy bunny battery ads. They keep going and going with no social life whatsoever. They're the work robots of the world, so it's best to be on top of your work as much as possible and communicate sooner rather than later!

3. The Micromanager: These people are perfectionists who get super nitpicky about the slightest detail. This is due to a lack of trust, leading to the consistent habit of hovering over someone's shoulder like they're a child. To battle these kinds of bosses, *Business News Daily* suggests going into it with a "no-surprise philosophy." Communicate always, no matter how big or small the details are.

4. The Cheerleader: This person always wants to see you grow and succeed no matter what. They are there for you in and outside the office. Working for this type of boss requires some boundaries depending on the relationship, but be respectful in all communication. Always aim to keep a consistent schedule, communication, and work ethic around them. These types of bosses are keepers.

5. Independence Is Key: This boss likes to keep things light and let you be free. This is the complete opposite of the micromanager. Keep this person in check with goal progress, concerns, and questions. They're not there to hold your hand every step of the way, so it's always good to learn something from each experience.

6. Traditionalist: This person wants to always have everything in check and keep it original. This one isn't necessarily a bad one to encounter, but know that they might

not be doing 360 changes anytime soon. With this type of boss, it's super important to be on time for every meeting and work independently.

7. M.I.A. Boss: This boss is literally missing in action, as ABC7 Chicago would say.[44] No matter how many messages or notifications you send about feedback or follow-ups, they never seem to answer you. Unfortunately, people still do this. It's nothing against you but about how they communicate. It's always important to keep them in the loop. And I know this is hard, especially for type-A people, but wait for them to respond. If it's been a couple of days without any updates, follow up. If it continues to be a problem, talk to them about it without being critical because they are still your boss.

8. Harmony: This boss wants to empathize and create connections in the workplace. Their motto is to guide their employees in the right direction and understand all parts of them. *Entrepreneur* suggests that you keep your emotions in check, be able to receive honest feedback, and be willing to build strong connections with your colleagues.[45]

9. Marathon Bosses: These people are going full speed ahead, whether it's a decision on what they want for lunch or a project proposal. They're quick on their feet and expect you to be just as fast as they are. To keep up with a fast-paced boss, have your ducks in a row. While reading a LinkedIn article, I found that they can be impatient if you

---

44 Jessica Shaeffer, "How to deal with different types of bosses," ABC7 News.
45 Rose Leadem, "6 Types of Bosses and How to Work With Them (Infographic)," *Entrepreneur.*

don't have a decision or task completed.[46] Keep everything in check and make sure you're getting everything done in a timely manner.

10. "There's No I in Team" Boss: These kinds of bosses want to be right there with you working together. No job is too small for them. It will always be a team effort, which gives everyone a chance to have equal say during the process. To please this boss, according to Indeed, it's always best to collaborate frequently with other colleagues and keep each action thoughtful.[47] Their top priority is for everyone and the company to succeed.

Now that we've gone through all ten types of bosses, we'll explore how to be a successful work bee no matter which field you pursue.

Learning about your own communication style:

Whether it's through email or phone calls, a good communication style will lead to future roles and promotions. Think about it. How would you feel if someone wasn't communicating a lot? It hurts, and it leaves you anxious to know what's going on. Please don't be that person.

In an interview with Adzaan Mutquir, a freelance graphic designer and fashion queen, we talked about communication tips and tricks. She was into remote work before it became a common theme for the pandemic. She initially started her freelance journey for a jewelry owner as a freshman in college.

---

46   Rachel Parnes, "4 Boss Types—and How to Work with Them," LinkedIn (blog), January 27, 2020.

47   "Five Types of Bosses, Which One Are You?", *Indeed*.

She was extremely grateful for that exposure early in her college experience.

"I'm so happy I did that; I'm so happy that was my first opportunity, working remote internships a lot. It teaches how communication styles work and how you need to really be independent in your work. You don't have the same structure; you have to be forced to create your own structure."

By putting herself out there and not knowing remote work, she ended up learning a lot more early on about her communication style as well as effectively keeping others, including her boss, in the loop. What I truly enjoyed about listening to Adzaan's experience is how she was real about her initial communication style. It not only showed how she learned through those experiences but how everyone reading this book can learn and adapt to those essential skills.

Here are some of the best tips to be a great communicator:

1. It's better to over-communicate than under-communicate: This saves a bunch of time if there is a problem early on. Your boss and colleagues will appreciate you even more if you update them on projects or tasks. No notification is too small. Keeping everyone updated = good office ethic and chill vibes.
2. Sooner rather than later approach: When I worked as a newspaper writer, I was fresh out of my sophomore year and trying to schedule an interview. However, I did it later in the week and got yelled at over the phone for not letting them know sooner. I was so upset because the person didn't react in the best way, and I could have definitely

said something earlier, looking back. I learned from that moment on to communicate earlier so people can plan ahead and prepare. No one likes a last-minute scrambler.

3. Keep yourself accountable: Always keep yourself in check. I use Google Calendar and list to get things done. If you make a mistake, take that as a learning opportunity and move on to the next thing. It's a bad look if you can't take criticism, and it's a lot of wasted energy if you can't move past it.

4. Try to respond during a reasonable time during the work window from 8:30 a.m. to 5 p.m. This creates boundaries of balancing work and free time while keeping it professional on both ends. Don't keep a person waiting if they're relying on your feedback. Try to do it in the morning so you can move on to the bigger tasks afterwards.

Overall, communication is a two-way street. Do what's best for you while thinking of the people on the other end. Learning how to balance the two early on will make you an excellent communicator and future boss! It will never go unnoticed.

When I got my first job, it was really amazing, especially during the pandemic. I was so excited to meet everyone. Although it was very different from an in-person setting, as a team, we made the best connections. The best thing I learned is that connections are unbreakable. No matter where you are in the world, connections are crucial to maintain and worth making the effort to stay in touch.

Here are some of the ways to follow coworker etiquette:

1. Personality tests are my savior and can be yours: This should be done right away so you can determine your mindset style and those of other people you're working with. Such tests make it better to work together and understand each person right off the bat!

2. Put yourself in their shoes and vice versa: Always consider where a person is mentally and physically. Play it by ear and see where they are each week. If they're struggling with something, consider how you can help them. It's about considering another person's perspective and listening to them fully.

3. Teamwork makes the dream work: I mentioned this earlier in the different types of bosses, but it also applies to colleagues you're actively engaging with. Delegating can be tricky, but balancing the workload not only makes the work stronger but brings in a collaborative environment to obtain different opinions.

The many coworkers you come across will be different each time, but it's important to be genuine and understanding while balancing your needs as well. This will build you up toward success and help you work with the next person. Also, if there are conflicts with other coworkers, it's best to have an open, honest conversation with them. If something isn't working or you need more clarification, it's better to do it sooner rather than later.

These qualities, personalities, and work ethics don't happen right away. It's a process of understanding each of your qualities as a worker bee and how to work alongside other people. Sometimes those experiences aren't ideal, but they are sometimes necessary to grow and know when to stand up for yourself aside from the position. Don't be too hard on yourself if you don't know exactly what to do. All these things take time and happen for a reason. No effort you make will go unnoticed and will go a long way if you learn these qualities ahead of time.

CHAPTER 14

CAREER PIVOTS

———

The toughest part is adapting to change within your career path. Especially when you're about to graduate, you will be forced to make many new changes. This year's pandemic also challenged many people's career paths. I attended the Built By Girls Second Summit, and we all took a poll on what we were all anxious about this year. Most of us were afraid of the future and what's to come.

I'm glad I wasn't the only one feeling that anxiety. However, acknowledging what we're feeling and having the tools at the tips of our fingertips was the most impactful. Now it's definitely not an easy experience, but each time you go through it, you get stronger and wiser.

My former coworker and dear friend, Betty Jean, started dipping her toes into influencer marketing and social media (which is taking off more and more each day) while balancing grad school.

She started as a political science and public policy major but knew in her heart it wasn't for her. Now, before we get deeper into this discussion, get your notepad ready because the pivot/social media queen is speaking some words of wisdom.

> *"My biggest motivator right now is chasing a lifestyle. I am chasing a lifestyle that I would like to currently live [...] I am chasing a lifestyle so that one day when I have a family, I'm able to give them everything that they want and that I am able to give."*

Even if you don't have all the clear answers yet, you must understand your values and goals. No need to get technical yet. Just know that it's a normal part of the process to deal with the uncertainty of it all. This includes balance within your aura.

In the Built By Girls virtual event, I got a chance to listen to guest speaker Amanda Seales, comedian and creative visionary. Her background entails a hit series on HBO called *Insecure*, where she plays the character Tiffany DuBois. She also runs a successful weekly podcast and wrote a book called *Small Doses*. This series is about truth-telling that can be used in daily life. During the event, she gave such amazing insight into mental wellness and how prioritizing your health is your armor. I admired that she referred to those aspects in a positive light because often it can be seen as a weakness when it actually gives you more space to be successful. Therapy often goes into that negative headspace, which is unfortunate because it's such a great tool to center yourself. But Amanda put this new perspective of therapy perfectly regarding stressful situations in career pivots:

"It's not to be stigmatized anymore. Therapy should be something that you're very openly talking about, and it really should be something that you consider cool. At this point when I hear someone talk about going to therapy, I know that's a different kind of person. My judgment of that person levels up because that was a person being responsible about their wellness. When you're responsible for your own wellness, that is a sign of how you're responsible in the world, because you're taking care of yourself, which means you are going to be a better addition to this society," said Amanda.

I truly admired this perspective. As I was growing up, I always had a lifestyle coach to guide me through my anxiety. When I was younger, I was always ashamed of it. I thought it made me more of a freak since it was stigmatized and was "uncool" if you had to talk to someone about your problems. Looking forward to the present, I'm actually grateful for it. Taking the time to talk to someone who isn't family about problems and ideas, especially within career pivots, gives you a new perspective of the situation.

I listened to another speaker, Soledad O'Brien—journalist, speaker, author, and philanthropist. She is one of the current anchors and producers of the Hearst Television political magazine *Matter of Fact with Soledad O'Brien*. Soledad discussed her experiences of choosing resilience over rejection. When she worked for CNN, people in the office asked if she was okay, only it was a lot more people than expected. Then one of her close colleagues told her she was about to get fired soon since she heard it through the grapevine. Nervous, she talked about it with her husband afterward. Then they went over a thoughtful, emotionless game plan for each scenario so there was more forward-thinking. The next day, she was called into her boss's office and there was an unexpected turn of events:

> *"It was very different from the experience that I had early on in my career. I wasn't blindsided; I wasn't a mess. I remember it wasn't fun, and certainly it wasn't pleasant, but it was like: Huh, I thought through this. I have actually thought through this very scenario. I said to him, "Well, why don't we go have lunch and talk about what we should be doing next?" And it was in that conversation that I was able to negotiate staying on as an anchor but overseeing the document. So essentially, I got a promotion out of that. And a lot of it was because I wasn't a complete mess. In fact, in a way, the power came to me and he was a little unnerved by it."*

Life can be full of surprises. Soledad took that conversation into a pivotal moment, and that's what you need to do for yourself. Advocating for yourself is putting your all in it with either success or failure, but it can be a very rewarding process. If she hadn't gone into it with a game plan and calmly asked for a discussion, she wouldn't have gotten promoted. That was crucial for her career pivot.

The rejection of being let go is sometimes hard to come to terms with. It's even harder when it's your first time being let go, whether it's your decision to leave your job or not. I left my first job recently, the one I got during the pandemic. The company was getting rebranded in the fall. There was some miscommunication about the position during that transition, so I decided not to work for the company anymore. Everyone was amazing, but I knew it was time to pursue other interests. Sending my final email to my boss was bittersweet. I was excited to pursue other ventures post-grad, but I knew I would miss the memories that came with working there. I learned so much throughout that time and made connections that will last into my career. It was my first job ever. I'll forever be grateful for those experiences and meeting my former colleagues along the way.

If you're in the process of quitting or just got let go, here are some tips:

1. Acknowledge how you're feeling: It's totally normal to feel bad no matter which end of the spectrum you're on. Do what makes you feel most comfortable to release that energy into the world. When I left my first job, I called my mom and told her what was going on. I acknowledged how I was feeling while looking forward to that discussion. You definitely don't want to bottle up those emotions, and it's necessary to let that news sink in for at least a day or two to get back on your feet faster.

2. Leave on good terms: I've met people who have said incredibly nasty things online about their job or internship experience and bosses. That is not the way to go about things, especially for future work. Even if the experience wasn't ideal, always thank the person for the opportunity and say good riddance in private. For my former boss's birthday, I texted her a nice note because there was no beef and we still had a good vibe. I never want to burn a bridge or leave something where I'm being rude. Always

put your best foot forward and stay in touch with people because you never know where it could lead.

3. Don't give up: Something will come through and you'll get the job. The more times you put yourself out there, the more likely you'll succeed.

4. Get your finances in check: This is definitely not my strong suit because I'm more creative. However, my whole family and inner circle has always taught me about budgeting, being money smart, and the basics of finances. It's not that bad; I promise. Sorting out your finances and budget is most important for getting back into the job world with confidence. I added some helpful suggestions for beginners:

   a. Use an Excel sheet or app to keep track of your expenses.

   b. Know that every month will vary.

   c. Saving is your best friend.

   - I'm sorry, girl, but you can't go on that shopping spree yet! Better to save your money for when you need it the most.

   d. Differentiate your wants and needs.

      - MoneyWise explains this best: "It can be hard to say 'no,' especially to the people who are closest to us.[48] But making a commitment to what you will and won't spend on is **making a commitment to your own values.**"

   e. Save the change and extra money you make along the way.

5. Update and practice your skills: If it's been a while since you've updated your resume or interview skills, don't

---

48 Rona Richardson, "Women Share Vital Money Advice They Wish They Knew Sooner," MoneyWise, September 20, 2019.

sweat it. There are plenty of resources that can help you in the process. I usually visit LinkedIn to learn some tips, and I love going to networking events or workshops. Nowadays, it's easier than ever to find something online that best suits your needs. You're never too old or "experienced" to go to one, and you'll always learn something new each time.

6. Negotiate your departure and whether you qualify for unemployment benefits: According to Glassdoor, it's better to go over this after you hear the news.[49] Negotiate the maximum severance pay and health insurance info if your company provided those benefits in the past.

7. Mentally prepare yourself for those conversations: Thinking about and discussing why you were let go is unavoidable. It will come up whether it's with a close friend or someone interviewing you. Practicing what you're going to say is a great tip from Indeed.[50] They also suggest practicing those answers in a positive light. Never bash the company, boss, or colleagues. That definitely will burn a lot of bridges and future opportunities.

8. Get a good reference: This can be your boss, colleague, or someone higher up you've been close to. As long as it's a viable option, then they should be willing to help you toward your future pursuits. Bustle says that "no matter what, you want to leave any job with a good reference."[51]

9. Ask for feedback: As much as it's hard to accept the reality of it all, asking for feedback on your performance will

49 Lilian Childress, "7 Things to Do Immediately if You Get Fired," *Glassdoor, Career Advice*, February 26, 2019.

50 "What To Do After Getting Fired," *Indeed*, December 24, 2020.

51 Dasha Fayvinova, "17 Things To Do After You've Been Fired Or Let Go," *Bustle*, last modified May 3, 2016.

benefit you. Refinery29 suggests that this can make a positive step toward self-improvement and analyzing each of your experiences so you can do things differently in your next job.[52]

10. Breathe and give yourself a break: Giving yourself time to move forward and accept the current situation will make things better in the long run. Keep in mind that it's not forever. It's only a temporary moment in time that you'll grow from.

This isn't easy to go through because it means you are an adult experiencing every part of life. It's good to have these experiences even though they are difficult. It's a sign of big and better things coming your way and teaching yourself how to roll with the punches. To all the grads, to all the people who just left their job, to all the people who just got terminated, everything will work out. Know that you're not alone in this. You have a community of people who love and appreciate everything you do. A company will appreciate those qualities of hard work, ambition, and persistence. I believe you'll find something amazing.

---

52 Judith Ohikuare, "8 Things To Do The Week After You're Laid Off," *Refinery29*, last modified March 21, 2018.

CHAPTER 15

STARTING YOUR OWN BUSINESS

—

Within the small business spectrum, I believe the most exciting chapter begins when you finally start the process of creating and marketing your company. You start to fantasize about the potential and the success of your business growing with utter happiness and confidence. However, a lot goes into small business plans before success comes. To get a better perspective and understanding, I talked to a few small business owners and gathered the biggest takeaways to grow a company you're passionate about.

Brooke Sheridan, founder and creator of Nuri Collective, began her small business journey during her college career. Initially, she went to Ohio University for a couple of years and transferred to Ohio State while studying graphic design and visual communications. However, she found that the original plan to graduate college wasn't her cup of tea anymore. This decision was based on what felt right to her.

"I wanted to be doing something creative and hands-on and know myself completely for the work that I was doing. So I thought, I just have to do it. I don't know if this will be the best decision. I don't know where this is going to go, but if I drop out, things completely fail; I have zero sales. I can always go back to school," said Brooke.

After consulting with her family, Brooke had a better idea of what she wanted to do and made her final decision. She decided to continue her journey with her Etsy shop to showcase and sell her digital prints while continuing freelance work. Later, after her digital prints became popular, Brooke decided to go into jewelry making, and the Nuri brand empire was born. This experience not only allowed her to grow but also allowed her to make decisions for herself.

1. TAKE THE TIME FOR YOU

While Brooke was telling me her story, I was on the edge of my seat. I couldn't even imagine doing something so ballsy because it's such a big, life-changing decision. **Brooke, if you're reading this, props to you! You stayed true to who you are and stuck with what's right for you!**

This is just one of the many examples of what it means to be your own girlboss. This story shows why it's so important to understand yourself first before creating your own brand. In life, you may not know what's right or wrong in terms of the future, but the time is now to make decisions that are right for you. It's not about what other people are doing or thinking but about determining how you feel about your current decisions and plans moving forward. It's okay if something doesn't feel right! We're all human. Whenever you think something's impossible, check again. The word impossible says "I'm possible." Cheesy, but it's true.

2. STARTS WITH AN O...ENDS WITH AN D...CAN YOU GUESS WHAT I'M TALKING ABOUT?

Now keep in mind, this is only the beginning of the process. Learning the ropes and finding the right steps can be overwhelming. But now it's time for something important. Can you guess? If you said, "Get organized," you're right!

I sometimes struggle with this because having a bunch of to-dos can be nerve-wracking. My anxiety goes up when I talk about *to-do* anything. We all sometimes want to have eight arms and do everything at once, but we were only blessed with two arms on this planet.

However, there are ways we can manage the stress while balancing everything. Let's start with five Ws and H, which stand for Who, What, When, Where, Why, and How. I initially learned this while studying journalism, but I love this structure because it can apply to anything.

Even if you don't know all the answers yet, at least write down a few goals or a vision of where you'd like to be. I'm a firm believer in putting out what you want in the world, and sometimes you have to be your own cheerleader to build yourself. It can be beneficial to see your vision come to life while also making your goals come true. The five Ws and H will indeed get you far in your career journey.[53]

Sophia Blasi, founder of Urban Luxe, has a recommendation for people wanting to start a business.

> *"Start with a business plan. I never did because I didn't think I would get this far. But I definitely think that's important for the money aspect of it, like planning out how much you're going to spend. Money is a big thing, just budgeting and finding the best deals and just paying attention to how much you're spending."*

Even though finance isn't everyone's forte, it's important, especially for funding and managing your own business. That's the time to be nitpicky and tedious so that you're aware of all aspects of your business.

3. KNOWING THE REALITY OF THE HUSTLE

I talked to one of my very good friends, Kaxi Novales, about her experience running a small business while balancing school and life. She owns Oxford Made, and she graduated from Miami University. When we first met, I was a brand rep for her company. I'd never done something like this before, so I was pretty nervous. But when I met her, she truly inspired me. I could tell right off the bat she was confident in herself and her company and was ambitious. I absolutely

---

53 Tara Monosoff, "8 Tips to Get Your Business Going, Even if You Don't Know Where to Start," *Entrepreneur.*

loved it. She told me something interesting that I never really thought of before.

> "*I remember I lived in an environment that was super rough, and it was constantly. Just how do I do it, how do I make X amount of money in order to get out of where I was born. I was resourceful and thought, Oh, I am pretty creative, I'm good at drawing, and I'm going to make stuff. And I have craft supplies, and it's more realistic.*

Usually, when people create businesses, it's for a creative outlet in their lives, but Kaxi had to do it to keep a steady flow of money. I truly respect the hustle because sometimes you don't hear stories about that. It's mostly about success stories, which is not a bad thing. However, you should keep in mind that, when it comes to success, the struggle is what makes it happen. It's where you learn most about yourself and what you need to do in order to be your best self.

You can have many reasons for your why, which is why I thought Kaxi's example was a great representation. Sometimes starting a business isn't all glitz and glamour in the beginning, but it's the hustle behind it that shapes your community and your brand.

4. FINDING YOUR WHY

Recently, I caught up with an old friend who started her own business. We met at the Girlboss Rally in California when she was selling her jewelry in between sessions. I bought a ring myself, and she made them like no other. Kate Davis, founder and creator of Knockout Inc., dedicated her passion for jewelry to provide women with a fashionable accessory while being able to defend themselves if ever in a sticky situation. Researchers estimate that approximately 20 percent of women in the United States have been sexually assaulted.[54] Acquaintances assaulted at least three-quarters of these women, while strangers attacked approximately one-quarter of them.

The worst fear is getting your car, you're by yourself, and your car is parked in a dark, eerie parking lot with only a few dim lights that absorb into the darkness. As you're walking, you see only the faintest shadow following you across as you walk toward your car. Then, as you're quickly going about your way, you hear footsteps. Your gut tells you something is wrong, but you keep walking, hoping they will go away, but they don't. They keep going faster, faster, faster until you're left scared, running for your life to escape.

"I would say almost every person I spoke with told me that they had put keys between their fingers when they were walking to their car. I had no idea that was something other people did too. I think our moms or whoever your caregiver is teaches you to do these things. Or you do it out of instinct and then you're like, Okay, this is just me feeling nervous when I'm walking to my car, or wherever you're going. I had so many women at these events tell me that they also felt nervous in car parking

---

54 "Sexual Assault of Women by Strangers Guide No. 62 (2011)," Arizona State University.

*lots. They were like, 'What a brilliant idea. Why
doesn't something like this exist? We're all carrying
our keys and there's nothing beyond pepper spray.'
There's no other product that women carry on their
hands that makes them feel good," Kate said.*

That is only the tip of the iceberg of what women can face if
we aren't in a safe area. If this insight doesn't set the scene
for women's safety, I don't know what will. From talking to
Kate and other women about their experiences, I know I'm
not the only woman who has struggled with this type of
situation before. It's honestly a really scary feeling knowing
that we are sometimes vulnerable. It's the main reason Kate
started her own business dedicated to protecting women to
ensure we each have something to protect ourselves with.

Even though this is more of a serious example of finding your
why, it reflects aspects about the feelings you have toward your
company, what others think of it, what you want to instill
within your company values, and how you can make the
world a better place with your company's platform. Having
those thoughts jotted down can make the biggest difference.

When you know your why, the process of becoming your own
boss manifests. Being your own boss ties into the imposter
syndrome chapter, but it is absolutely relevant in today's age.
As women are currently making our way to leadership roles
and fighting for gender equality, they are now stepping up to
the plate and making money moves. When you are your own
boss, it can be nerve-racking. Being your own boss doesn't
necessarily mean one aspect, but it means taking control of
your life whether you own a company or not.

CONCLUSION

———

Being independent, being confident, and being persistent are qualities that take time. Putting yourself out there can be tough on top of evolving into your best self. However, it's not impossible. All it takes is persistence and time.

Sometimes it can be overwhelming. Sometimes I wish there was a switch to have all the good things at once or a magical fairy who can make my wishes come true. It's realizing you have the potential to be the next leader in your pursuits.

Sometimes it can seem too crazy to think about what the future could hold.

For example, if you told my younger self that I would be writing and finishing a book during my early twenties, I would've thought you were crazy. In reality, persisting through any setback or challenge is possible. Changing your mindset can be a challenge within itself. Before turning in my copy edits, I was battling a bad case of COVID-19. Talk about a walking nightmare. Even though it was totally unexpected,

I pushed through because I saw the glass as half full instead of half empty.

You might not know what will come next, but can I tell you a secret? Picture this.

You are the main character in this story. No one else is in control but you. You may not know what will happen next, but the story will guide you to your happy ending. Sure, there will be twists and turns. However, we forget that bad moments realistically don't last that long. Sometimes all you need is a little nudge in the right direction to know that you'll be okay and to flip the switch. It takes time to shift your mindset to this concept; I know from my own experience.

Yet I know enjoying the ride makes the journey more enjoyable and memorable in the long run. Thinking of yourself as the main character in your timeline is crucial because it's true. Act like it.

It's about finding ways to stay true to your values while acknowledging the work of progress you've completed and are progressing towards. In the past, I've dealt with my own challenges of saying sorry too much and having a bad habit of procrastination.

Having a mindset is key to leveling up in your life, but it's also about balancing authenticity within yourself. Throughout this writing process, my hope is that this book has given you guidance into your own happily ever after. Contact me if it has; I'd love to know.

ACKNOWLEDGEMENTS

———

Thank you for being the first people to preorder my book and for supporting me throughout this process. I'm so grateful for you all and sending hugs to each and every one of you!

Giulia Baldini

Lucy Cox

Charlie Cox

Tilar Delvine

Derek Feilmeier

John Grad

Caroline Haubenstricker

Michelle Hill

Brian Johnson

Erik Koester

Ellie Krug

Jennifer Lee

Bruce Keebeck Lee

Lauren Lee

Fiona Mckenna

Stephanie McKibben

Richard Michalik Jr.

Ali Michalik

Becky Minger

Adzaan Muqtadir

Jordan Podojil

Bridget Ryan

Brooke Sheridan

Grace Yoo

APPENDIX

CHAPTER 1

Fahkry, Tony. "Why Success Involves Going From Failure To Failure Without Losing Enthusiasm." *Medium.* July 8, 2018. https://medium.com/the-mission/why-success-involves-going-from-failure-to-failure-without-losing-enthusiasm-b7f18acc759c.

Goalcast. "Deshauna Barber: One Question Changed Her Life Forever." August 3, 2019. Video, 6:08. https://www.youtube.com/watch?v=7BRrvPQzTwE&list=LLgM4fDLKsJPlSWQcoARpR7Q&index=2768.

Jacimovic, Darko. "18 Eye-Opening College Student Stress Statistics." *What To Become.* February 10, 2021. https://whattobecome.com/blog/college-student-stress-statistics/#:~:text=20%25%20of%20students%20report%20going,issues%20as%20the%20main%20stressor.

Ouellette, Coral. "FOMO Statistics You Need to Grow Your Business." *TrustPulse.* October 23, 2019. https://trustpulse.com/

fomo-statistics/#:~:text=General%20FOMO%20Statistics&-text=56%25%20of%20people%20who%20experience,hour%20 without%20checking%20social%20media.

Uzzi, Brian. "Research: Men and Women Need Different Kinds of Networks to Succeed." *Harvard Business Review.* February 25, 2019. https://hbr.org/2019/02/research-men-and-women-need-different-kinds-of-networks-to-succeed.

Zalis, Shelley. "Power Of The Pack: Women Who Support Women Are More Successful." *Forbes.* March 6, 2019. https://www. forbes.com/sites/shelleyzalis/2019/03/06/power-of-the-pack-women-who-support-women-are-more-successful/?sh=-2faf11e11771.

CHAPTER 2

Jordan, Alexander H. et al. "Misery Has More Company Than People Think: Underestimating the Prevalence of Others' Negative Emotions." *Personality and Social Psychology Bulletin* 37, no. 1 (January 2011): 120–35.

Miller, Jenesse. "COVID-19-fueled anxiety and depression peaked in early April, then declined." June 4, 2020. https:// news.usc.edu/171124/anxiety-depression-covid-19-mental-distress-usc-survey/.

CHAPTER 3

Pace, Natalie. "The First Female CEO of a Television Network Offers a Springboard for Other Women." *Huffington Post.*

December 6, 2017. https://www.huffpost.com/entry/the-first-female-ceo-of-a_b_3558422.

Patel, Deep. "8 Ways to Stay Accountable With Your Goals." *Entrepreneur Magazine*. March 6, 2019. https://www.entrepreneur.com/article/328070.

CHAPTER 4

Abrams, Allison. "8 Steps to Improving Your Self-Esteem." *Psychology Today*. March 27, 2017. https://www.psychologytoday.com/us/blog/nurturing-self-compassion/201703/8-steps-improving-your-self-esteem.

Bunchman, Meghan Anne. Broadcast Your Beauty: TV Tips and Series. Monee. White Feather Press. 2020. 1–118.

Campbell, Leigh. "4 In 5 Women Have Low Self Esteem. Here's What We Can Do About It." *Huffington Post*. August 2, 2016. https://www.huffingtonpost.com.au/2016/08/01/four-in-five-australian-women-have-low-self-esteem_a_21443099/.

Winch, Guy. "5 ways to build lasting self-esteem." *TED TALK X*. August 23, 2016. https://ideas.ted.com/5-ways-to-build-lasting-self-esteem/.

CHAPTER 5

Bilbray, Sandra "Never Second-Guess Yourself Again." *LiveHappy*. March 18, 2016. https://www.livehappy.com/self/never-second-guess-yourself-again?nopaging=1.

Blakeman, Steve. "5 Simple Ways to Quiet Your Annoying Inner Voice." *Inc. Magazine.* August 26, 2017. https://www.inc.com/ steve-blakeman/5-simple-ways-to-silence-your-annoying-inner-voice.html.

Firestone, Lisa. "Steps to Overcoming Your Critical Inner Voice." *Psychology Today.* May 21, 2010. https://www.psychologytoday.com/us/blog/compassion-matters/201005/steps-overcoming-your-critical-inner-voice.

Ingraham, Christopher. "People who second-guess themselves make worse decisions, study finds." *The Washington Post.* https://www.washingtonpost.com/business/2020/01/06/people-who-second-guess-themselves-make-worse-decisions-study-finds/.

Manning-Schaffel, Vivian. "Here's how to stop second-guessing yourself all the time." NBC News. https://www.nbcnews.com/ better/lifestyle/here-s-how-stop-second-guessing-yourself-all-time-ncna1128681.

Mejia, Zameena. "3 pieces of career advice Girlboss founder and CEO Sophia Amoruso wants you to know." *CNBC.* https:// www.cnbc.com/2017/11/06/3-pieces-of-advice-girlboss-founder-sophia-amoruso-wants-you-to-know.html.

Sherman, E. Jeremy. "Ten Tips For People Who Second-guess Themselves." *Psychology Today.* Aug 19, 2015. https://www. psychologytoday.com/us/blog/ambigamy/201508/ten-tips-people-who-second-guess-themselves#:~:text=Second%2D-guessing%20can%20be%20bad,us%20easily%20into%20 self%2Ddoubt.

"Ways to Stop Second-guessing Yourself." *Bustle.* Last modified June 5, 2016.

"3 Signs that Self-Doubt is Getting in Your Way." *Thrive Global.* Updated February 22, 2019.

CHAPTER 6

Itani, Omar. "8 Quotes By Ghandi That Will Change The Way You Think." *Medium, Mind Cafe.* Feb 20, 2020. https://medium.com/mind-cafe/8-quotes-by-gandhi-that-will-change-the-way-you-think-e7b4599c0be1.

CHAPTER 7

Chu, Melissa. "Why Your Brain Prioritizes Instant Gratification Over Long-Term Goals, According to Science." *Inc. Magazine.* July 10, 2017.

Masicampo, E. J. and Roy F. Baumeister. "Consider It Done! Plan Making Can Eliminate the Cognitive Effects of Unfulfilled Goals." 1–18.

CHAPTER 9

Giang, Vivian. "You can teach yourself to be a risk-taker." *BBC News.* June 6, 2017. https://www.bbc.com/worklife/article/20170606-you-can-teach-yourself-to-be-a-risk-taker?referer=https%3A%2F%2Fquip.com%2F.

Hill, Brian. "The Importance of Planning in an Organization." *Chron News.* February 12, 2019. https://smallbusiness.chron.com/importance-planning-organization-1137.html.

McRoberts, Sam. "Here's What Science Says You Should Do to Achieve Greater Success." *Entrepreneur Magazine.* December 29, 2017. https://www.entrepreneur.com/article/305985#:~:-text=Taking%20risks%20eliminates%20the%20possibility,their%20olives%20because%20of%20it.

Rampton, John. "Businesses That Took Huge Risks That Paid Off." *Inc. Magazine.* October 11, 2016. https://www.inc.com/john-rampton/15-businesses-that-took-huge-risks-that-paid-off.html.

Sturt, David and Todd Nordstrom. "4 Reasons Why Asking For Help Makes You A Stronger, Not Weaker, Leader." *Forbes Magazine.* November 7, 2017. https://www.forbes.com/sites/davidsturt/2017/11/01/4-reasons-why-asking-for-help-makes-you-a-stronger-not-weaker-leader/?sh=7360a40d3c1a.

Warner, Jennifer. "Are Risk Takers Happier?" *WebMD.* September 19, 2005.

CHAPTER 10

Blake, Jenny. "When To Make A Career Pivot." *Forbes Magazine.* September 9, 2016. https://www.forbes.com/sites/nextavenue/2016/09/09/when-to-make-a-career-pivot/?sh=474330d17e0b.

"How to Adapt to Change in the Workplace." *Indeed, Career Guide.* Last modified December 10, 2020.

O'Connor, Caroline and Perry Klebahn. "The Strategic Pivot: Rules for Entrepreneurs and Other Innovators." *Harvard Business Review.* February 28, 2011.

CHAPTER 11

(@businesswifey). "Never tiptoe through life babygirl. Let them hear every step you take." Instagram photo. October 14, 2020.

Hoare, Rose. "How seeing the big picture could bring success, fulfillment." *CNN.* August 30, 2012.

Joshi, Olly. "29 Ways To Remind Yourself To Keep Sight Of Life's Bigger Picture." Elite Daily. February 10, 2014. https://www.elitedaily.com/life/motivation/29-ways-to-remind-yourself-to-keep-sight-of-lifes-bigger-picture.

Geldart, Phil. "The Importance of Seeing the Big Picture." *Entrepreneur Magazine.* April 30, 2020. https://www.entrepreneur.com/article/349368.

Tovar, Virgie. "Meet One Of The Original Plus Size Influencers." *Forbes Magazine.* October 13, 2020. https://www.forbes.com/sites/virgietovar/2020/10/13/meet-one-of-the-original-plus-size-influencers/?sh=3cf8bc545156.

CHAPTER 12

Expert Panel, Forbes Human Resources Council. "14 Effective Ways To Stand Out From Other Applicants." *Forbes Magazine*. June 15, 2020. https://www.forbes.com/sites/forbeshumanresourcescouncil/2020/06/15/14-effective-ways-to-stand-out-from-other-applicants/?sh=3feffe-a227bb.

Haselmayr, Melanie. "5 Creative Ideas To Make Your Job Application Stand Out." *Forbes Magazine*. September 5, 2013. https://www.forbes.com/sites/allbusiness/2013/09/05/5-creative-ideas-to-make-your-job-application-stand-out/?sh=439e74252b1f.

CHAPTER 13

"Five Types of Bosses, Which One Are You?" Indeed.

Huhman, Heather H. "15 Types Of Bosses And How To Work For Them." *Business Insider*. June 3, 2013.

Leadem, Rose. "6 Types of Bosses and How to Work With Them (Infographic)." *Entrepreneur Magazine*. https://www.entrepreneur.com/article/299176.

Parnes, Rachel. "4 Boss Types—and How to Work with Them." *LinkedIn (blog)*. January 27, 2020. https://www.linkedin.com/business/learning/blog/career-success-tips/4-boss-types-and-how-to-work-with-them.

Shaeffer, Jessica. "How to deal with different types of bosses." ABC7 News. https://abc7chicago.com/boss-bad-bosses-different-types-of/5600178/.

CHAPTER 14

Childress, Lilian. "7 Things to Do Immediately if You Get Fired." *Glassdoor, Career Advice.* February 26, 2019.

Fayvinova, Dasha. "17 Things To Do After You've Been Fired Or Let Go." *Bustle.* Last modified May 3, 2016.

Ohikuare, Judith. "8 Things To Do The Week After You're Laid Off." *Refinery29.* Last modified March 21, 2018.

Richardson, Rona. "Women Share Vital Money Advice They Wish They Knew Sooner." *MoneyWise.* September 20, 2019. https://moneywise.com/a/women-share-the-practical-money-advice-they-wish-they-knew-sooner.

"What To Do After Getting Fired." *Indeed.* December 24, 2020.

CHAPTER 15

Monosoff, Tara. "8 Tips to Get Your Business Going, Even if You Don't Know Where to Start." *Entrepreneur Magazine.* https://www.entrepreneur.com/article/207488.

"Sexual Assault of Women by Strangers Guide No. 62 (2011)." Arizona State University.

Made in the USA
Monee, IL
28 July 2021

74092549R00095